ENGLISH

T0182353

Verbs &

Essentials
of Grammar
for ESL Learners

Ed Swick

Mc Graw Hill

New York Chicago San Francisco Lisbon London Madrid Mexico City
Milan New Delhi San Juan Seoul Singapore Sydney Toronto

The McGraw·Hill Companies

Library of Congress Cataloging-in-Publication Data

Swick, Edward.
　　English verbs & essentials of grammar for ESL learners / by Ed Swick.
　　　　p.　cm.
　　ISBN 0-07-163229-8
　　　1. English language—Textbooks for foreign speakers.　　2. English language—
　　Grammar—Problems, exercises, etc.　　3. English language—Verb—Problems,
　　exercises, etc.　　I. Title.　　II. Title: English verbs and essentials of grammar for ESL
　　learners.

　　PE1128.S9776　　2009
　　428.2'4—dc22　　　　　　　　　　　　　　　　　　　　　　　　2009013545

7 8 9 10 11 12　QVS/QVS　20 19 18 17 16

ISBN　978-0-07-163229-4
MHID　　0-07-163229-8

McGraw-Hill books are available at special quantity discounts to use as premiums and
sales promotions or for use in corporate training programs. To contact a representative,
please e-mail us at bulksales@mcgraw-hill.com.

This book is dedicated to my terrific grandchildren: Riane, Aaron, and Riley Swick and Jalyn and Tori Cox.

Contents

Preface

English Verbs & Essentials of Grammar for ESL Learners is a practical guide and handbook for the student of English who wants a quick reference on verbs and grammar. The purpose of the book is to present and illustrate the major concepts of the language that are the basis for speaking, understanding, reading, and writing with accuracy.

Part 1 of the book is devoted to verbs. Although English does not have complicated conjugational forms, English verbs have a variety of tenses and specific uses for certain tenses that must be understood to use verbs appropriately. This book presents the various tenses with clarity and provides an abundance of examples that illustrate the use of the tenses and how different kinds of verbs function in those tenses. The last chapter of Part 1 illustrates the formation and function of phrasal verbs, an English concept that is often a mystery to nonnative speakers. The language used in the examples throughout the book is authentic and contemporary.

Verb usage and tenses are summarized in Appendix A, which gives an overview of all verb types and their functions, illustrated in a series of useful tables. Appendix B provides a complete list of irregular verbs and the formations they take in the past tense and as past participles. Each appendix serves as a guide to quick answers to the most commonly posed questions about verbs.

Part 2 of the book is a review of all aspects of English grammar, from the use of definite and indefinite articles to the rules for sentence construction and punctuation. It is a convenient reference for finding explanations of difficult points of grammar. These explanations are accompanied by appropriate examples that use current, high-frequency expressions. Each chapter in Part 2 presents a single grammar topic, which allows for an in-depth look at the target subject of the chapter. Just like Part 1 of *English Verbs & Essentials of Grammar for ESL Learners*, Part 2 uses language that is simple and concise, which makes the book practical for English students of any level of proficiency.

Students of English will find this a helpful handbook for review or even as an introduction to new concepts. It is a valuable and handy tool for travel, business, and individual or classroom study.

Part I

English Verbs

1. The Present Tense

The English present-tense conjugations are relatively simple to form. There are three distinct types of present-tense conjugations:

1. The simple present tense, which indicates a habitual or repeated action

2. The progressive, which indicates an ongoing or incomplete action

3. The emphatic response

The Simple Present Tense

The simple present tense of most verbs requires only an -*s* ending in the third-person singular. This is true whether the subject is a pronoun (*he, she, it*) or a singular noun. The first- and second-person pronouns (*I, we, you*), the third-person plural pronoun (*they*), and plural nouns require no ending in the present tense of this type:

Subject	*to help*	*to run*	*to put*
I	help	run	put
you	help	run	put
he/she/it	helps	runs	puts
we	help	run	put
they	help	run	put
the boy	helps	runs	puts
the boys	help	run	put

This tense shows a habitual or repeated action:

I always help my friends. (*always* = I help my friends all of the time.)
He runs the fastest. (It is his habit to run the fastest.)
They put salt on the sidewalk after it snows. (This habit occurs after every snow.)

When negating verbs in the simple present tense, the auxiliary *to do* followed by the adverb *not* is required. They both precede the negated verb:

Tom does not understand.   We do not care anymore.
Bill doesn't like her.   I don't speak Russian.

There are only two English verbs that have a more complex conjugation in the simple present tense:

Subject	*to be*	*to have*
I	am	have
you	are	have
he/she/it	is	has
we	are	have
they	are	have
the boy	is	has
the boys	are	have

These two verbs also show a habitual or repeated action. Note that adverbs are used to accentuate that meaning:

I am a student at this school. (My regular activity is being a student.)
They are seldom home. (Their occasional habit is to be away from
    home.)
She often has toast for breakfast. (Her habit is to have toast for
    breakfast.)
I have five brothers. (These boys are my brothers every minute of
    every day.)

When negating *to be*, the adverb *not* follows the conjugated form of *to be*. When negating *to have* as a transitive verb, a form of *to do* is required followed by the adverb *not*:

This is not my idea of fun.
I do not have your documents.
We aren't alone in this room.
Mark doesn't have any change.

Auxiliaries

Most auxiliaries do not require an ending in the third-person singular conjugation, except those that are derived from a transitive verb or those formed with the verb *to be*. The auxiliary *must*, for example, never has an ending; the auxiliary *to want to* comes from a transitive verb and requires a third-person singular ending; and the auxiliary *to be able to* is formed with the verb *to be*:

Subject	*must*	*to want to*	*to be able to*
I	must	want to	am able to
you	must	want to	are able to
he/she/it	must	wants to	is able to
we	must	want to	are able to
they	must	want to	are able to
the boy	must	wants to	is able to
the boys	must	want to	are able to

When auxiliaries such as these are used with another verb, the other verb is in its infinitive form. The conjugated verb in the sentence is the auxiliary. For example:

He **must explain** his behavior. (auxiliary with no ending)
Bill **can help** you with this project. (auxiliary with no ending)
No one **wants to go** to his party. (auxiliary with third-person singular ending)
Mary **likes to sing** and **dance**. (auxiliary with third-person singular ending)
We **are able to communicate** with them. (auxiliary formed with *to be*)
She **is supposed to arrive** at noon. (auxiliary formed with *to be*)

When negating auxiliaries, the three types of auxiliaries follow different patterns:

1. Auxiliaries that have no third-person singular conjugational change (*must, can,* for example) are simply followed by the adverb *not.*

You must not lie to me.
She cannot hear you.
That shouldn't matter.
It can't be true.

2. Auxiliaries that also function as transitive verbs (*want to, like to,* for example) use *to do* plus *not* to form the negative.

I do not want to complain.
Tim does not like to surf anymore.
We don't want to stand in your way.
She doesn't like to sit in the back row.

3. Auxiliaries that are formed with the verb *to be* (*to be able to, to be supposed to,* for example) place the adverb *not* after the verb *to be.*

I am not able to reach the switch.
You aren't supposed to touch that.

The Progressive Conjugation

The progressive conjugation is composed of a present-tense conjugation of the verb *to be* and an accompanying verb formed as a present participle (*singing, making, talking,* and so on). It is only the verb *to be* that requires any conjugational changes in the present tense. The present participle is static:

Subject	*to help*	*to run*	*to put*
I	am helping	am running	am putting
you	are helping	are running	are putting
he/she/it	is helping	is running	is putting
we	are helping	are running	are putting
they	are helping	are running	are putting
the boy	is helping	is running	is putting
the boys	are helping	are running	are putting

This tense shows an action that is in progress and not yet complete. It is often incomplete because of an interruption:

I am helping Tom. (My helping Tom is an ongoing task.)
She is running in a race. (At this moment, she is in a race and not yet at the finish line.)
Bill is putting milk in the glass when he breaks the glass. (This action is interrupted by the glass's being broken.)

The verbs *to be* and *to have* can also be used in this tense form:

Subject	*to be*	*to have*
I	am being	am having
you	are being	are having
he/she/it	is being	is having
we	are being	are having
they	are being	are having
the boy	is being	is having
the boys	are being	are having

The usage of *to be* and *to have* in this tense form indicates an action in progress or interrupted:

You are being very stubborn. (Your stubbornness is ongoing.)
They are having a party when the lights go out. (The party is interrupted by the sudden darkness.)

When negating progressive verbs with *not*, the adverb is placed between the verb *to be* and the present participle:

I am not listening.
She is not studying.
We aren't going.
Tom isn't joining us tonight.

The Emphatic Response

An emphatic response is used as a *contradiction* to what someone else has stated—positive or negative. If the statement is positive, the emphatic response is negative. If the statement is negative, the emphatic response is positive. The auxiliary verb *to do* is used together with another verb to form the emphatic response:

I do like broccoli.
We don't have a car.

In response to a negative statement, use the positive form of *to do*:

They don't help us.	That's not true. They **do** help us.
Mary doesn't sing in our chorus.	She **does** sing in our chorus.

In response to a positive statement, use the negative form of *to do*. Notice that a form of *to do* is not required in positive statements, except those that use *to do* as a transitive verb and not as an auxiliary:

They live on Main Street.	No. They don't live on Main Street.
You need my advice.	I don't need your advice!
Tom does his chores alone.	Tom doesn't do his chores alone.

If an emphatic response to a sentence in which the verb is in the progressive form is needed, the auxiliary *to do* cannot be used. Instead, in speech the auxiliary *to be* or the negative adverb is intoned, and in writing, the response can end with an exclamation point:

She isn't listening.	She **is** listening!
We aren't going along.	You **are** going along!
You are being foolish.	I am **not** being foolish!
Jim is staying in the city.	Jim is **not** staying in the city!

Questions

Only the simple present tense and the progressive formation in the present tense can be stated as questions. The emphatic response does not occur as a question; it is only used to reply to a previously made statement. However, its characteristic use of the auxiliary *to do* becomes important in the formation of many questions in the simple present tense.

Most verbs in a simple present-tense sentence can be used to ask a question by means of the auxiliary verb *to do*. If the subject of the sentence is a third-person singular pronoun or noun, the verb becomes *does*. With all other persons, the verb becomes *do*:

Present-Tense Statement	Present-Tense Question
John speaks two languages.	**Does** John speak two languages?
They swim laps daily.	**Do** they swim laps daily?
She respects Professor Jones.	**Does** she respect Professor Jones?
The women earn enough money.	**Do** the women earn enough money?

If the verb in the present-tense statement is the transitive verb *to have*, the question formed from the verb can often begin with the verb itself or be formed together with the auxiliary *to do*:

Present-Tense Statement	Present-Tense Question
You have an answer to the question.	**Have** you an answer to the question?
	Do you have an answer to the question?
She has a valid passport.	**Has** she a valid passport?
	Does she have a valid passport?

If the verb in the present-tense statement is the verb *to be*, the question begins with the verb itself:

Present-Tense Statement	Present-Tense Question
I am well again.	**Am** I well again?
There is a problem here.	**Is** there a problem here?
The workers are angry.	**Are** the workers angry?

Since the progressive present tense requires the use of the verb *to be*, the approach to question formation for *to be* is used:

Present-Tense Statement	Present-Tense Question
Mother is sitting alone.	**Is** mother sitting alone?
The crops are growing well.	**Are** the crops growing well?
I am confusing you.	**Am** I confusing you?

If an auxiliary is derived from a transitive verb (*want*, *like*, *have*, and so on), it forms questions with the verb *to do*:

Present-Tense Statement	Present-Tense Question
She wants to stay here.	**Does** she want to stay here?
We do not have to get up early.	**Don't** we have to get up early?

Auxiliary verbs can be used with all three types of present-tense conjugations. When they are used, the meaning of the conjugational type is retained. For example:

He rides his bike to school. (His habit is to ride his bike to school.)
He **has to** ride his bike to school. (His "compulsory" habit is to ride his bike to school.)

She is swimming laps. (She is in the process of swimming laps.)
She **might** be swimming laps. (Someone suggests she may be swimming laps.)

You don't like yogurt.	I **do** like yogurt! (emphatic response)
Mary can't speak French.	Mary **can** speak French! (emphatic response)

Modal Auxiliaries

Modal auxiliaries are auxiliaries that change the nuance of the meaning (*obligation*, *desire*, and so on) of an accompanying verb. The modals that are followed by an infinitive that omits the particle word *to* are:

can	might
could	must
had better (better)	should
may	would

Those that include the particle word *to* in the infinitive are:

be able to	like to
be allowed to	need to
be supposed to	ought to
be to	used to
have got to	want to
have to	wish to

When modal auxiliaries are used in the present tense, they become the verb that is conjugated in a sentence. The accompanying verb is always in the form of an infinitive—one that represents a habitual or repeated action or one that represents an action in progress. For example:

Habitual or Repeated Actions
I can understand both English and German.
We must always help our neighbors.
You have got to be on time from now on.
They often want to spend the night at Aunt Jane's house.

Action in Progress
Tim may be playing in tomorrow's game.
Should you be looking through your sister's purse?
She is supposed to be studying in her room.
John needs to be earning more money.

2. The Past Tense

The English past-tense conjugations consist of two forms that also exist in the present tense:

1. The simple past tense, which indicates a habitual, repeated, or complete action
2. The progressive, which indicates an ongoing or incomplete action

The Simple Past Tense of Regular Verbs

The simple past tense of most verbs requires an *-ed* ending with regular verbs. No other conjugational endings are needed for any of the persons in either the singular or plural:

Subject	*to help*	*to pull*	*to call*
I	helped	pulled	called
you	helped	pulled	called
he/she/it	helped	pulled	called
we	helped	pulled	called
they	helped	pulled	called
the boy	helped	pulled	called
the boys	helped	pulled	called

This tense shows a habitual, repeated, or complete action:

I always helped my friends. (*always* = I helped my friends all of the time.)
He often pulled a red wagon. (It was his habit to pull a red wagon.)
They called me every day. (*every day* = They called me repeatedly.)

The Simple Past Tense of Irregular Verbs

Irregular verbs form the simple past tense in more than one way. Some make a vowel change. Some make a vowel and consonant change. A few transform completely. And a small group of verbs in the past tense looks identical to the present-tense verb:

Subject	*to know*	*to buy*	*to go*	*to put*
I	knew	bought	went	put
you	knew	bought	went	put
he/she/it	knew	bought	went	put
we	knew	bought	went	put
they	knew	bought	went	put
the boy	knew	bought	went	put
the boys	knew	bought	went	put

Although these verbs have an irregular formation in the simple past tense, they still show a habitual, repeated, or complete action.

> Bob knew him in grade school. (a habit throughout grade school)
> I always bought American cars. (*always* = My habit was to buy American cars.)
> Jane went home. (complete action)
> She put on lipstick every day. (a habit every day)

There are two English verbs that require a special look in the simple past tense:

Subject	*to be*	*to have*
I	was	had
you	were	had
he/she/it	was	had
we	were	had
they	were	had
the boy	was	had
the boys	were	had

These two verbs also show a habitual, repeated, or complete action. Note that adverbs are used to accentuate the habitual or repeated meaning:

> I was a student at this school. (My regular activity was being a student.)
> They were seldom home. (Their occasional habit was to be away from home.)
> She often had toast for breakfast. (Her habit was to have toast for breakfast.)
> I had five dollars. (complete action = I no longer have the money.)

When negating verbs in the simple past tense, the auxiliary *did* followed by the adverb *not* is required for most verbs. They both precede the negated verb:

Tom did not understand.
We did not care anymore.
Bill didn't like her.
I didn't speak with her.

When negating *to be*, the adverb not follows the past-tense form of *to be*. When negating *to have* as a transitive verb, *did* is required followed by the adverb *not*:

This was not my idea of fun.
I did not have your documents.
We weren't alone in the room.
Mark didn't have any change.

Auxiliaries

Not all auxiliaries can be formed in the past tense. The auxiliary *must*, for example, uses an auxiliary with a synonymous meaning for the past tense:

must   had to

The auxiliary *can* has a past-tense form but can also use an auxiliary with a synonymous meaning as its past tense:

can   could or was able to

Auxiliaries that are also used as transitive verbs (for example, *to want* or *to like*) can change to the past tense. Auxiliaries that are formed with the verb *to be* (for example, *to be able to*) change the verb *to be* to the past tense:

Subject	*may*	*to want to*	*to be able to*
I	might	wanted to	was able to
you	might	wanted to	were able to
he/she/it	might	wanted to	was able to
we	might	wanted to	were able to
they	might	wanted to	were able to
the boy	might	wanted to	was able to
the boys	might	wanted to	were able to

When an auxiliary is used with another verb, the other verb is in its infinitive form. The conjugated verb in the sentence is the auxiliary. For example:

He **had to explain** his behavior.
Bill **could help** you with this project.

No one **wanted to go** to his party.
We **were able to communicate** with them.
She **was supposed to arrive** at noon.

When negating auxiliaries, the three types of auxiliaries follow different patterns.

1. Auxiliaries such as *might* and *could* are simply followed by *not*:

You might not agree with me.
She could not hear you.

2. Auxiliaries that also function as transitive verbs (*want to, like to,* for example) use *did* plus *not* to form the negative:

I did not want to complain.
Tim did not like to surf anymore.
We didn't want to stand in your way.
She didn't like to sit in the back row.

3. Auxiliaries that are formed with the verb *to be* (*to be able to, to be supposed to,* for example) place the adverb *not* after the verb *to be*.

I was not able to reach the switch.
You weren't supposed to touch that.

See a complete list of irregular past-tense forms in Appendix B at the end of the book.

The Progressive Conjugation

The progressive past tense is composed of a past-tense conjugation of the verb *to be* and an accompanying verb formed as a present participle (*singing, making, talking,* and so on). It is only the verb *to be* that requires any conjugational changes in the past tense. The present participle is static:

Subject	*to help*	*to run*	*to put*
I	was helping	was running	was putting
you	were helping	were running	were putting
he/she/it	was helping	was running	was putting
we	were helping	were running	were putting
they	were helping	were running	were putting
the boy	was helping	was running	was putting
the boys	were helping	were running	were putting

This tense shows an action that was in progress or was not yet completed. It is often incomplete because of an interruption:

I was helping Tom. (My helping Tom was an ongoing task.)
She was running in a race. (She was in a race but may not have finished it.)
Bill was putting milk in the glass but dropped the glass. (This action
   was interrupted by the glass's being dropped.)

The verbs *to be* and *to have* can also be used in this tense form:

Subject	to be	to have
I	was being	was having
you	were being	were having
he/she/it	was being	was having
we	were being	were having
they	were being	were having
the boy	was being	was having
the boys	were being	were having

The usage of *to be* and *to have* in this tense form indicates an action that
was in progress or interrupted:

You were being very stubborn. (Your stubbornness was ongoing.)
They were having a party when the lights went out. (The party was
   interrupted by the sudden darkness.)

When negating progressive verbs with *not*, the adverb is placed between
the verb *to be* and the present participle:

I was not listening.
She was not studying.
We weren't going.
Tom wasn't joining us tonight.

Questions

Both the simple past tense and the progressive formation of the past tense
can be stated as questions. The auxiliary *did* is frequently used in the construction of questions.

Most verbs in a simple past-tense sentence can be used to ask a question
by means of the auxiliary verb *did*:

Past-Tense Statement	Past-Tense Question
John spoke two languages.	**Did** John speak two languages?
They swam laps daily.	**Did** they swim laps daily?
She respected Professor Jones.	**Did** she respect Professor Jones?
The women earned enough money.	**Did** the women earn enough money?

If the verb in the past-tense statement is the transitive verb *to have*, the question formed from the verb can often begin with the verb itself or be formed together with the auxiliary *did*:

Past-Tense Statement	Past-Tense Question
You had an answer to the question.	**Had** you an answer to the question?
	Did you have an answer to the question?
She had a valid passport.	**Had** she a valid passport?
	Did she have a valid passport?

There is a tendency to form questions with the verb *to have* by means of a form of the verb *to do*. If the verb in the past-tense statement is the verb *to be*, the question formed from the verb begins with the verb itself:

Past-Tense Statement	Past-Tense Question
He was sick again.	**Was** he sick again?
There was a problem here.	**Was** there a problem here?
The workers were angry.	**Were** the workers angry?

Since the progressive past tense requires the use of the verb *to be*, the approach to question formation for *to be* is used:

Past-Tense Statement	Past-Tense Question
Mother was sitting alone.	**Was** mother sitting alone?
They were planting corn.	**Were** they planting corn?
It was confusing you.	**Was** it confusing you?

If an auxiliary is derived from a transitive verb (*want, like, have*, and so on), it forms questions with the verb *did*:

Past-Tense Statement	Past-Tense Question
She wanted to stay here.	**Did** she want to stay here?
We did not have to get up early.	**Didn't** we have to get up early?

Auxiliary verbs can be used with both types of past-tense conjugations. When they are, the meaning of the conjugational type is retained. For example:

He rode his bike to school. (His habit was to ride his bike to school.)
He **had to** ride his bike to school. (His "compulsory" habit was to ride his bike to school.)

She was swimming laps. (She was in the process of swimming laps.)
She **was supposed to** be swimming laps. (It was presumed that she was swimming laps.)

The type of past-tense question formed with auxiliaries depends upon the type of auxiliary and whether the action is complete or in progress. If the auxiliary is also a transitive verb and indicates a complete action, the question begins with *did*. If the auxiliary is formed with *to be* or is in the progressive form, the question begins with *was/were*:

He had to go to school.	**Did** he have to go to school?
She was supposed to go home.	**Was** she supposed to go home?

When such questions are negated, *did* begins the question and the adverb *not* follows the subject. If the adverb is formed as a contraction, it is attached to the auxiliary *did*. If the auxiliary is formed with *to be*, the question begins with *was/were* and not *did*:

He did not have to go to school.	**Did** he not have to go to school?
I didn't want to help.	**Didn't** you want to help?
They were not able to attend.	**Were** they not able to attend?
She wasn't supposed to go home.	**Wasn't** she supposed to go home?

3. The Present Perfect and the Past Perfect

The English perfect-tense conjugations consist of two forms that also exist in the present tense. They occur in both the present perfect and the past perfect tense:

1. The simple perfect tenses, which indicate a habitual, repeated, or complete action

2. The progressive perfect tenses, which indicate an ongoing or incomplete action

The Perfect Tenses of Regular Verbs

The perfect tenses require an *-ed* ending on past participles formed from regular verbs. The past participles are preceded by *has* or *have* in the present perfect tense and by *had* in the past perfect tense. No other conjugational endings are needed for any of the persons in either the singular or plural:

Subject	*to help*	*to pull*	*to call*
I	have/had helped	have/had pulled	have/had called
you	have/had helped	have/had pulled	have/had called
he/she/it	has/had helped	has/had pulled	has/had called
we	have/had helped	have/had pulled	have/had called
they	have/had helped	have/had pulled	have/had called
the boy	has/had helped	has/had pulled	has/had called
the boys	have/had helped	have/had pulled	have/had called

The present perfect and past perfect tenses show a habitual or repeated action. A verb in the present perfect tense indicates an action begun in the past and completed in the present. A verb in the past perfect tense indicates an action begun and completed in the past:

I have always helped my friends. (*always* = I have helped my friends all of the time.)

He had often pulled a red wagon. (It had been his habit to pull a red wagon.)

They have called me every day. (*every day* = They have called me repeatedly.)

She had worked here since June. (Her work began in June and ended later in the past.)

The Perfect Tenses of Irregular Verbs

Irregular verbs form past participles in more than one way. Some make a vowel change. Some make a vowel and consonant change. A few transform completely. And a small group of verbs as past participles looks identical to the present-tense verb. All use *have*, *has*, or *had* as their auxiliary:

Subject and Auxiliary	*to make*	*to know*	*to buy*	*to go*	*to put*
I have/had	made	known	bought	gone	put
you have/had	made	known	bought	gone	put
he/she/it has/had	made	known	bought	gone	put
we have/had	made	known	bought	gone	put
they have/had	made	known	bought	gone	put
the boy has/had	made	known	bought	gone	put
the boys have/had	made	known	bought	gone	put

Although these verbs have an irregular past participle, they still show a habitual or repeated action:

I have always bought American cars. (*always* = My habit has been to buy American cars.)

Bob had known him in grade school. (a habit throughout grade school)

She has put on lipstick. (complete action)

Jane had gone home. (complete action)

There are two English verbs that require a special look in the perfect tenses:

Subject	*to be*	*to have*
I	have/had been	have/had had
you	have/had been	have/had had
he/she/it	has/had been	has/had had
we	have/had been	have/had had
they	have/had been	have/had had
the boy	has/had been	has/had had
the boys	have/had been	have/had had

These two verbs also show a habitual, repeated, or complete action. Note that adverbs can be used to accentuate the habitual or repeated meaning:

They have rarely been here. (Their rare habit has been to be here.)
I had been a student at this school. (My regular activity had been being a student.)
I have had a flat tire. (complete action = having had a flat tire)
She had often had toast for breakfast. (Her habit had been to have toast for breakfast.)

When negating verbs in the perfect tenses, the auxiliary *have* followed by the adverb *not* is required. They both precede the past participle:

Tom has not understood.	We had not heard the news.
Bill hasn't been in the army.	She hadn't yet arrived.
Mother has not been well.	I hadn't had enough sleep.

Modal Auxiliaries

Not all modal auxiliaries can be formed in the perfect tenses. The auxiliary *must*, for example, uses an auxiliary with a synonymous meaning for the present perfect and past perfect:

must → have had to / had had to

The auxiliary *can* has no perfect-tense form but can also use an auxiliary with a synonymous meaning to form the perfect tenses:

can → have been able to / had been able to

Modal auxiliaries that are also used as transitive verbs (for example, *to want* or *to like*) can change to the perfect tenses. Auxiliaries that are formed with the verb *to be* (for example, *to be able to*) change the verb *to be* to a participle (*been*). Both types use *have/had* as their auxiliary:

Subject	*want to*	*to be able to*
I	have/had wanted to	have/had been able to
you	have/had wanted to	have/had been able to
he/she/it	has/had wanted to	has/had been able to
we	have/had wanted to	have/had been able to
they	have/had wanted to	have/had been able to
the boy	has/had wanted to	has/had been able to
the boys	have/had wanted to	have/had been able to

When a modal auxiliary is used with another verb, the other verb is in its infinitive form. The auxiliary in the sentence is conjugated in the perfect tenses. For example:

He **has had to explain** his behavior.
Bill **had been able to help** you with this project.
No one **has wanted to go** to his party.
We **had been able to communicate** with them.

If the perfect tenses sound awkward with auxiliaries (for example, *he has been supposed to go* . . .), the past tense is used instead (*he was supposed to go* . . .).

When negating modal auxiliaries used in the perfect tenses, just like other perfect-tense phrases, the adverb *not* or other negative follows the auxiliary verb *have/had*:

I have not wanted to complain.   Tim had never liked to ski.
We haven't been able to move.   She had never been allowed to travel.

See a complete list of irregular participial forms in Appendix B at the end of the book.

The Progressive Conjugation

The progressive perfect tenses are composed of *have been*, *has been*, or *had been* and an accompanying verb formed as a present participle (*singing*, *making*, *talking*, and so on). It is only the progressive auxiliary that requires any conjugational changes in these tenses. The present participle is static:

Subject and Auxiliary	*to help*	*to run*	*to put*
I have/had been	helping	running	putting
you have/had been	helping	running	putting
he/she/it has/had been	helping	running	putting
we have/had been	helping	running	putting
they have/had been	helping	running	putting
the boy has/had been	helping	running	putting
the boys have/had been	helping	running	putting

This tense shows an action that has been in progress or has not yet been completed. It is often incomplete because of an interruption:

I have been helping Tom. (My helping Tom has been an ongoing task.)
She had been running in a race. (She had been in a race but may not have finished it.)

Bill had been putting milk in the glass but dropped the glass. (This action had been interrupted by the glass's being dropped.)

When negating progressive verbs with *not*, the adverb is placed between the verb *have/had* and *been*:

I had not been listening.
We haven't been working.

She has not been studying.
Tom hadn't been lending a hand.

Questions

Both the simple perfect tenses and the progressive formation of the perfect tenses can be stated as questions. In both cases, the auxiliary *have/had* begins the question:

Perfect-Tense Statement	Perfect-Tense Question
John has learned two languages.	**Has** John learned two languages?
They had been swimming laps.	**Had** they been swimming laps?
She had respected Professor Jones.	**Had** she respected Professor Jones?
They have been earning money.	**Have** they been earning money?

Modal auxiliary verbs can be used in perfect-tense formations, but the verb that follows the modals will be in its infinitive form. For example:

He has ridden his bike to school. (His habit has been to ride his bike to school.)
He **has had to ride** his bike to school. (His "compulsory" habit has been to ride his bike to school.)

She has learned to dance. (a complete action)
She **has been able to learn** to dance. (She has had the ability to learn to dance.)

When sentences in the perfect tenses that contain a modal auxiliary are formed as questions, the auxiliary *have/had* begins the question and is followed by the subject, the modal auxiliary, and the remainder of the sentence:

Has he had to ride his bike to school?
Has she been able to learn to dance?
Had the men wanted to work all day?
Had they been allowed to cross the border here?

When such questions are negated, the adverb *not* follows the subject. If the adverb is formed as a contraction, it is attached to the auxiliary *have/had*:

Has he not had to ride his bike to school?
Hasn't she been able to learn to dance?
Had the men not wanted to work all day?
Hadn't they been allowed to cross the border here?

4. The Future and the Future Perfect

The English future tense describes an action that will take place at some future time. The English future perfect tense describes an action that will begin and be completed at some future time. The future and future perfect-tense conjugations consist of two forms that also exist in the present tense:

1. The simple future and future perfect, which indicate a habitual, repeated, or complete action

2. The progressive future and future perfect, which indicate an ongoing or incomplete action

The Simple Future Tense

Since the simple future tense is formed from a combination of the auxiliaries *will* or *shall* with an infinitive, there is no complication when using regular or irregular verbs, because irregularities do not occur in infinitives. In formal style, the first-person singular and plural use the auxiliary *shall*, and the other persons use the auxiliary *will*. But in less formal style, *will* is used with all persons and will be used here. Let's look at the simple future-tense conjugation:

Subject	*to help*	*to pull*	*to be*
I	will help	will pull	will be
you	will help	will pull	will be
he/she/it	will help	will pull	will be
we	will help	will pull	will be
they	will help	will pull	will be
the boy	will help	will pull	will be
the boys	will help	will pull	will be

The future tense shows a habitual or repeated action carried out at some time in the future. Adverbs of frequency often accompany this tense:

I will always help my friends. (*always* = I will help my friends all of the time.)
He will often pull her hair. (*often* = He will pull her hair frequently.)
They will be our new neighbors. (Their habit will be to be neighbors of ours.)

The Simple Future Perfect Tense of Regular Verbs

The future perfect tense is composed of the auxiliaries *will* or *shall* and a participial infinitive. A participial infinitive consists of the infinitive *have* followed by a regular past participle. Regular past participles end in *-ed* (*looked, stopped,* and so on):

Subject	*to call*	*to help*	*to try*
I	will have called	will have helped	will have tried
you	will have called	will have helped	will have tried
he/she/it	will have called	will have helped	will have tried
we	will have called	will have helped	will have tried
they	will have called	will have helped	will have tried
the boy	will have called	will have helped	will have tried
the boys	will have called	will have helped	will have tried

The future perfect tense shows a habitual or repeated action begun and carried out at some time in the future. Adverbs of frequency or that designate a time period in the future often accompany this tense:

Bill will sometimes have finished work early. (*sometimes* = "early" in the future)
I will have helped everyone by then. (*by then* = a time period in the future)
He will have tried every cake in the contest. (action begun and completed in the future)

The Future Perfect Tense of Irregular Verbs

Many past participles have an irregular formation. Some make a vowel change. Some make a vowel and consonant change. A few transform completely. And a small group of verbs as past participles looks identical to the present tense verb:

Subject and Auxiliary	*to make*	*to know*	*to buy*	*to go*	*to put*
I will have	made	known	bought	gone	put
you will have	made	known	bought	gone	put
he/she/it will have	made	known	bought	gone	put
we will have	made	known	bought	gone	put
they will have	made	known	bought	gone	put
the boy will have	made	known	bought	gone	put
the boys will have	made	known	bought	gone	put

Although the past participles are irregular, the simple future perfect tense functions in the same way as with regular past participles:

She will have made a thousand dollars. (action completed at a
    future time)
I will have bought a new car by Friday. (*by Friday* = a time period in
    the future)
Before you know it, they will have gone away. (*before you know it* =
    a time period in the future)

Modal Auxiliaries

Not all modal auxiliaries can be formed in the future or the future perfect tense. Where possible, they revert to another modal auxiliary with a synonymous meaning. For example:

must drive → will have to drive / will have had to drive
can drive → will be able to drive / will have been able to drive
should drive → will be supposed to drive / will have been supposed
    to drive

In some cases, the future perfect tense of a modal auxiliary sounds awkward. In such cases, the simple future tense can replace it.

When a modal auxiliary is used in the future or future perfect tenses, an accompanying irregular verb causes no complications, because it is the modal that is conjugated, and the accompanying verb always remains an infinitive. For example, in the future tense:

Subject	*to have to call*	*to be able to speak*	*to want to try*
I	will have to call	will be able to speak	will want to try
you	will have to call	will be able to speak	will want to try
he/she/it	will have to call	will be able to speak	will want to try
we	will have to call	will be able to speak	will want to try
they	will have to call	will be able to speak	will want to try
the boy	will have to call	will be able to speak	will want to try
the boys	will have to call	will be able to speak	will want to try

And in the future perfect tense:

Subject	*to have to call*	*to be able to speak*	*to want to try*
I	will have had to call	will have been able to speak	will have wanted to try
you	will have had to call	will have been able to speak	will have wanted to try
he/she/it	will have had to call	will have been able to speak	will have wanted to try
we	will have had to call	will have been able to speak	will have wanted to try
they	will have had to call	will have been able to speak	will have wanted to try
the boy	will have had to call	will have been able to speak	will have wanted to try
the boys	will have had to call	will have been able to speak	will have wanted to try

With the inclusion of a modal auxiliary in the future and future perfect tenses, these tenses still infer a habitual or repeated action at some time in the future. Adverbs of frequency or that designate a time period in the future often accompany these tenses:

He **will have to explain** his behavior.
Bill **will usually want to sit** on the porch after supper.
No one **will have been able to convince** him in time.
We **will have had to surrender** by dawn.

When negating these tenses, the adverb *not* follows the auxiliaries *will* and *shall*. The same pattern is used when modal auxiliaries are in the future or future perfect sentences:

I will not go out tonight.
Tom won't have found a new job by Tuesday.
We will not have to work tomorrow.
It won't be able to be fixed by then.

The Progressive Conjugation

The progressive future and future perfect tenses are composed of *will be* or *will have been* and an accompanying verb formed as a present participle (*singing, making, talking*, and so on). Since the auxiliary and participles that make up these tenses require no conjugational changes, all verbal elements in sentences are static:

Subject and Auxiliary	*to help*	*to run*	*to put*
I will be/have been	helping	running	putting
you will be/have been	helping	running	putting
he/she/it will be/have been	helping	running	putting
we will be/have been	helping	running	putting
they will be/have been	helping	running	putting
the boy will be/have been	helping	running	putting
the boys will be/have been	helping	running	putting

These tenses show an action that will be in progress or will not be completed. It is often incomplete because of an interruption. Let's look at the future tense first:

I will be helping Tom. (My helping Tom will be an ongoing task.)
She will be running in a race. (She will be in a race but may not finish it.)
Bill will be putting milk in the glass but will drop the glass. (This action will be interrupted by the glass's being dropped.)

Let's look at some examples with the future perfect tense:

She will have been working here for a year in June. (ongoing action = She will have had the job for a year in June but will continue working after June.)
On Sunday I will have been living here for three months, but because of an illness I have to return home on Saturday. (interruption = *because of an illness*)

It is technically possible to use modal auxiliaries in the progressive future and future perfect tenses. However, these tenses are full of verb forms and sound awkward. Therefore, the tendency is to use the simple tenses in place of the progressive tenses. For example:

Awkward: He will have to be riding his bike home.
Better: He will have to ride his bike home.

Awkward: I will have been able to be perfecting the formula before spring.
Better: I will have been able to perfect the formula before spring.

When negating progressive verbs with *not*, the adverb follows the auxiliaries *will* and *shall* as with the simple future and future perfect tenses:

I will not be joining you.
She won't be studying in Europe.
We will not have traveled to Maine.
They won't have arrived by tomorrow.

Questions

Questions in the future and future perfect tenses begin with the auxiliary *will* or *shall*. If the question is in the negative, *not* will follow the subject. If *not* is formed as a contraction with *will*, *not* precedes the subject:

Will John really learn a new language?
Will he not travel to Mexico City this year?
Will they have completed the dam before the start of winter?
Won't you have served as chairperson for three years?

If a modal auxiliary is part of the future or future perfect tense, the same pattern for questions occurs:

Will you have to learn the rules of the road?
Won't you want to go out with us tonight?

If the subject of a question in these tenses is *I* or *we*, *shall* is the preferred auxiliary unless the meaning implies that someone is wondering about the future:

Shall I help you with that?
Will I ever have a million dollars?

5. The Imperative

Most imperative statements, or commands, are given in the second-person singular or plural (*you*). The formation of a verb as an imperative is quite simple: remove the particle word *to* from the infinitive, and you have a command:

Go home.
Have fun.
Be happy.
Drive slowly.

If you change a statement to a command, the elements of the statement remain intact. It is only the verb that is altered. The *target* of that verb will always be second person, but the pronoun (*you*) is understood and not spoken or written. The tense of the verb is lost, and the verb becomes an elliptical infinitive (*to* is omitted). For example:

Statement: John came home by three o'clock.
Imperative: Come home by three o'clock.

Statement: She has been one of the candidate's supporters.
Imperative: Be one of the candidate's supporters.

Statement: We will help her look for her keys.
Imperative: Help her look for her keys.

Modal auxiliaries are not used in the imperative with the occasional exception of *to be able to*:

Be able to recite the Greek alphabet by tomorrow evening.

Imperatives can be softened or made to sound more courteous by adding the word *please* to them. This word is placed most often at the very beginning or the very end of the command:

Please stop by for a visit if you have time.
Please be on your best behavior.
Take a number and wait in line, please.
Have your tickets ready, please.

In many cases, in order to be brief, pat statements that are imperatives or that represent imperatives are used on signs or in general announcements over a loudspeaker. For example:

Deer Crossing (represents an imperative = Caution. Deer cross this road.)
Keep right except to pass. (roadside sign)
Merging Traffic (represents an imperative = Caution. Cars enter the highway here.)
No Parking (represents an imperative = Do not park here.)
No Smoking (represents an imperative = Do not smoke here.)
No Swimming (represents an imperative = Do not swim here.)
Post No Bills (an imperative = Post no signs on this wall.)
Reduce Speed Ahead (roadside sign)
Silence (represents an imperative = Be silent.)

Let's

It is possible to include the speaker or writer in an imperative. This is done by using *let's* (the contraction of *let us*) followed by an elliptical infinitive and complement. For example:

Let's talk about it. (We should talk about it.)
Let's make some lunch. (We should make some lunch.)
Let's ask Mary to help. (We should ask Mary to help.)
Let's take a trip to Spain. (We should take a trip to Spain.)

Because the speaker or writer is included in the imperative, the tone of the command is softened. The sound of the command is more courteous and less demanding. Even when the speaker or writer is aware that he or she is really not involved in the action of the verb, this form of command is used to sound more like a suggestion. Compare the following pairs of sentences:

Standard command: Try to be a little quieter.
***Let's* command:** Let's try to be a little quieter.

In the *let's* command illustrated above, the speaker or writer is suggesting that someone should be a little quieter and knows that the suggestion is only directed at the person to whom the command is given. The speaker or writer is only including himself or herself in order to make the command sound more like a suggestion. Another example:

Standard command: Remember to send Aunt Jane a birthday card.
***Let's* command:** Let's remember to send Aunt Jane a birthday card.

In the let's command, the speaker or writer is suggesting that someone should send Aunt Jane a birthday card and knows that the suggestion is only directed at the person to whom the command is given.

Let

The verb *let* can also be used to introduce a command, but the speaker or writer is not included in the command. Instead, a direct object follows *let*. The verb that describes the action of the command then follows the direct object. For example:

Let Jack cut the grass today. (direct object = *Jack*)
Let me use your car for the afternoon. (direct object = *me*)
Let the soldiers rest before the next march. (direct object = *the soldiers*)
Let her try on your new dress. (direct object = *her*)

Negating Imperatives

Most imperative sentences can be negated by introducing them with *do not* or *don't*. For example:

Positive: Stop the car in front of my house.
Negative: Don't stop the car in front of my house.

Positive: Stand on the edge of the cliff.
Negative: Do not stand on the edge of the cliff.

Positive: Be a member of their club.
Negative: Don't be a member of their club.

If the positive command begins with *let*, this use of *do not* or *don't* is still used:

Positive: Let him sign the contract.
Negative: Don't let him sign the contract.

Positive: Let his father shovel the snow from the driveway.
Negative: Do not let his father shovel the snow from the driveway.

A *let's* command does not follow this pattern. Instead, the adverb *not* follows the contraction *let's*:

Positive: Let's go shopping tomorrow.
Negative: Let's not go shopping tomorrow.

Positive: Let's help them paint the garage.
Negative: Let's not help them paint the garage.

Do for Emphasis

To make an imperative sound emphatic or to implore someone to carry out the action of the verb, an imperative sentence can be introduced by *do*:

Normal imperative: Come by for a visit some time.
Emphatic imperative: Do come by for a visit some time.

Normal imperative: Let's get together again next week.
Emphatic imperative: Do let's get together again next week.

Normal imperative: Let Mary try on the beautiful gown.
Emphatic imperative: Do let Mary try on the beautiful gown.

Suggestions and Recommendations

It is possible to state an imperative sentence as a suggestion or recommendation. This usually occurs when the speaker or writer does not wish to make the imperative sound like a demand. The verb in the suggestion or recommendation looks like an imperative verb. But it is not. In reality, the verb in the suggestion or recommendation is in the present subjunctive. Since the verb in the suggestion is a conjugated verb, the sentence must include a subject for that verb. (See Chapter 10 for the form and use of the English subjunctive.) Compare the following pairs of sentences:

Imperative: Be on time tomorrow.
Suggestion: I suggest you be on time tomorrow. (subject = you)

Imperative: Take a couple days off from work.
Suggestion: We recommend she take a couple days off from work. (subject = she)

Imperative: Have the operation soon.
Suggestion: Dr. Jones suggested he have the operation soon. (subject = he)

Imperative: Memorize the poem.
Suggestion: Ms. Smith recommended Tom memorize the poem. (subject = Tom)

When the subject of such sentences is in the third-person singular, there is sometimes a tendency to provide the verb with the usual third-person singular -*s* ending. But that tendency must be avoided. A present subjunctive verb, which resembles an infinitive, is required. For example:

Typical statement: He **has** the operation.
Suggestion: The doctor suggested he **have** the operation.

Typical statement: She **arrives** on time.
Suggestion: I suggest she **arrive** on time.

This can be further illustrated with the verb *to be*:

Typical statement: She **is** more diligent.
Suggestion: I suggest she **be** more diligent.

Typical statement: I **am** less argumentative.
Suggestion: Tim suggests I **be** less argumentative.

Typical statement: You **are** the new chairperson.
Suggestion: She suggested you **be** the new chairperson.

If the imperative is in the negative, the sentence that is a suggestion or recommendation will include the adverb *not*:

Imperative: Don't be so angry.
Suggestion: I suggest you not be so angry.

Imperative: Don't let Mary get sick.
Suggestion: We recommend he not let Mary get sick.

6. Linking Verbs

Linking verbs *link* or *connect* the subject of a sentence with an adjective, noun, or pronoun that follows the linking verb. This occurs most frequently with the verb *to be*:

I am lonely.	We are teenagers.
You are correct.	You are the winner.
He is a soccer player.	They are careful.
She is a Baptist.	The man is a doctor.
It is you.	The girls are talented.

As the linking verb changes tenses, it has no effect on the other elements in the sentence:

Present: He is spoiled.
Past: He was spoiled.
Present perfect: He has been spoiled.
Past perfect: He had been spoiled.
Future perfect: He will have been spoiled.
Future: He will be spoiled.

In informal or casual style, it is common to use an objective-case pronoun after *to be*. In formal style, subjective-case pronouns are used. This is true in all tenses:

Subjective Case	**Objective Case**
That's he.	That will be him.
It was I.	It is me.

Other linking verbs work in the same manner as *to be*: they combine the subject of a sentence with an adjective that follows the verb. Some of these linking verbs can also be combined with nouns and pronouns that follow the verb. The verbs that are followed only by adjectives are:

appear	seem
feel	smell
grow	sound
look	stay
prove	taste

Each of these ten verbs can be followed by an adjective that modifies the subject of the sentence, and this can occur in any tense and with auxiliaries:

The man appears ill.
She feels unhappy.
The sky has grown dark.
His skin will look better tomorrow.
Their theory proves wrong.
The man seemed impatient.
The cookies smell so good.
The piano will sound better after tuning.
She wants to stay young.
The soup tasted delicious.

Two linking verbs (*to become* and *to remain*) can be followed by adjectives, nouns, and on rare occasions pronouns and can be used in any tense and with auxiliaries. For example:

The weather became awful. (adjective)
Betty wants to become a lawyer. (noun)
The lake remained calm. (adjective)
Bill hoped to remain an architect. (noun)

The verb *to seem* can sometimes be followed by a modified noun rather than just an adjective:

That seems a strange statement to me.

Some of the linking verbs can also be used as *transitive verbs*. That is, they do not combine a subject with an adjective that follows them, but, instead, they take a direct object. Compare the following sentences:

Linking Verb	Transitive Verb
She feels happy.	She feels **the fabric**. (direct object)
The cake smelled burned.	Bill smelled **the flowers**. (direct object)
It grows dark.	They grow **tropical plants**. (direct object)
The music sounds loud.	He sounds **the alarm**. (direct object)
It proved wrong.	She proved **the theory**. (direct object)
The soup tastes salty.	Mom tastes **the soup**. (direct object)

It is easy to determine whether these verbs are used as linking verbs or as transitive verbs. Replace the verb with an appropriate form of *to be*. If the sentence still makes sense, the verb is a linking verb. If it makes no sense, the verb is a transitive verb. For example:

Jim felt very lonely. → Jim **was** very lonely. (makes sense = linking verb)

Jim felt a pain in his arm. → Jim **was** a pain in his arm. (makes no
   sense = transitive verb)

The jam will taste sweet. → The jam **will be** sweet. (makes sense =
   linking verb)
I will taste the jam. → I **will be** the jam. (makes no sense =
   transitive verb)

The verb *to appear* must be mentioned specially. Although it does not
function as a transitive verb, it can be used as a verb that shows the *action of
appearing* and is in such a case not a linking verb. Compare the following
pairs of sentences:

She appeared refreshed and alert. (linking verb = *Refreshed* and *alert*
   modify *she.*)
A strange man appeared at the door. (action verb = *At the door* shows a
   location.)

He appears stunned by the news. (linking verb = *Stunned* modifies *he.*)
The same bird always appears at dawn. (action verb = *At dawn*
   expresses time.)

Something similar can occur with the verbs *to stay* or *to remain*:

Despite the pain, her smile stayed fixed on her face. (linking verb =
   Fixed modifies *smile.*)
John stayed in the tent. (action verb = *In the tent* shows a location.)

I remained confident. (linking verb = *Confident* modifies *I.*)
We remained at home last night. (action verb = *At home* shows a
   location.)

When *to be* Is Not a Linking Verb

It is important to remember that *to be* can act in several different ways: as
an auxiliary of other verbs, as part of the tense change of other verbs, or as
part of the passive voice. Some of the verbs in those structures can be linking verbs, and others can be transitive verbs.

When the progressive form of any tense of a verb is used, the presence of
to be is not an automatic signal that it is a linking verb. Let's look at some
examples:

Simple Tense	**Progressive Tense**
John is annoying.	John is being annoying.
	(linking verbs)
I was her friend.	I was being her friend.
	(linking verbs)

The leaves turned red.	The leaves were turning red. (linking verbs)
The solution proved wrong.	The solution was proving wrong. (linking verbs)
She will feel better.	She will be feeling better. (linking verbs)
Tom grows vegetables.	Tom is growing vegetables. (transitive verb)
He smelled her perfume.	He was smelling her perfume. (transitive verb)
I have appeared in a play.	I have been appearing in a play. (action verb)
They will help us.	They will be helping us. (transitive verbs)
Mike speaks French.	Mike is speaking French. (transitive verb)

If the sentence is in the passive voice, it must contain a transitive verb. Therefore, linking verbs are not included in passive sentences, although a form of *to be* does occur:

The soup is being served hot. (passive = *to be* + past participle)
That was discussed earlier. (passive = *to be* + past participle)
He has been severely punished. (passive = *to be* + past participle)
The problem will be solved by a committee. (passive = *to be* + past participle)

And although a form of *to be* occurs in the perfect tenses, it is not an automatic signal that a linking verb is being used:

Linking Verbs in the Perfect Tenses
Present perfect: Mary has been ill for some time.
Past perfect: He had appeared healthy just a week ago.
Future perfect: It will have grown dark by 7 P.M.

Transitive Verbs in the Progressive Perfect Tenses
Present perfect: James has been visiting us for a week.
Past perfect: I had been writing poems about her.
Future perfect: He will have been studying literature for a year by then.

When modal auxiliaries are used together with linking verbs, it is only the nuance of the meaning (*obligation, desire,* and so on) of the linking verbs that changes. The linking verbs are always in infinitive form when combined with modal auxiliaries. With some modals, the particle word *to* is omitted from the infinitive. They are:

Modal and Example Infinitive

can be	might appear
could seem	must feel
had better taste	should look
may grow	would prove

With other modal auxiliaries, the particle word *to* is included in the infinitive:

Modal and Example Infinitive

be able to stay	need to look
be allowed to grow	ought to stay
be supposed to be	used to taste
have got to sound	want to sound
have to appear	wish to seem
like to feel	

The use of modal auxiliaries in the various tenses can be found in Chapters 2, 3, 4, and 5.

7. Present Participles, Past Participles, and Verbals

Present Participles

Present participles are formed by adding *-ing* to the base form of a verb (*helping, seeing, coming,* and so on). Present participles have two functions: (1) They are used together with a form of *to be* to form the progressive tenses. (2) They can function as modifiers.

Present Participles in the Progressive Tenses
I am going to the store.
She was playing tennis with Tom.
They have been working all day on that project.
No one had been guiding them.
Mark will be visiting Mexico next month.
We will have been traveling four days by tomorrow.

See Chapters 1, 2, 3, and 4 for details on the progressive tenses.

Present Participles as Modifiers
The sleeping child seemed restless.
We observed the rapidly flowing river.
Her letter has a rather biting tone.
The dozing man didn't hear the bear approaching.

When a present participle is used as a modifier, it can stand before the noun it modifies, or it can stand behind the noun it modifies, especially when the present participle is part of a longer phrase. For example:

a working man   a man working long hours
running water   water running from a broken faucet
the singing girls   the girls singing a folk song

Because present participles are formed from verbs, adverbs can be used to modify present participles. If the present participle precedes a noun, the adverb will precede the present participle. If the present participle follows a noun, the adverb can precede or follow the present participle:

a carefully working man	a man carefully working / working carefully
slowly running water	water slowly running / running slowly
the loudly singing girls	the girls loudly singing / singing loudly

Past Participles

Past participles are used together with a form of the verb *to have* to form the perfect tenses: present perfect, past perfect, and future perfect. Past participles can be derived from regular verbs, which require the addition of the suffix *-ed* on the base form of a verb. Irregular past participles are formed in a variety of ways. Whether regular or irregular, both types of past participles function the same way in the three perfect tenses:

Regular Past Participle	Irregular Past Participle	Irregular Past Participle
have helped	have seen	have spoken
had helped	had seen	had spoken
will/shall have helped	will/shall have seen	will/shall have spoken

See Chapters 4 and 5 for details on the perfect tenses.

Like present participles, past participles can function as modifiers:

The stolen money was found in the attic.
Careful! That's a broken bottle.
The irrigated fields became fruitful.
Purified water is safe to drink.

If a past participle used as a modifier is accompanied by a longer phrase, it follows the noun it modifies:

the shattered glass	the glass shattered by his hammer
a repaired radio	a radio repaired last week
lost books	books lost on the way to school

Because past participles are formed from verbs, adverbs can be used to modify past participles. If the past participle precedes a noun, the adverb will precede the past participle. If the past participle follows a noun, the adverb can precede or follow the past participle:

the suddenly shattered glass	the glass suddenly shattered / shattered suddenly
a quickly repaired radio	a radio quickly repaired / repaired quickly
recently lost books	books recently lost / lost recently

Gerunds

Gerunds are *verbals* that are formed in the same way as present participles: the suffix *-ing* is added to the base form of a verb. But gerunds do not function in the same way as present participles. Gerunds are used as *nouns* that describe an action or a state of being. Compare the use of a gerund used as a noun and a standard noun:

Gerund	Noun
Swimming makes me tired.	Calisthenics make me tired.
Smoking is bad for you.	Cigarettes are bad for you.
Studying took effort.	The solution took effort.
Losing always hurts.	An injection always hurts.

Unlike standard nouns, gerunds are rarely preceded by a definite or indefinite article (*the, a, an*).

Since gerunds are nouns, they can be used like any other nouns: as the subject, the direct object, the subject complement, or the object of a preposition in a sentence. For example:

Subject: Jogging can be a healthy form of exercise.
Direct object: My family enjoys camping.
Subject complement: What Jane really likes is dancing.
Object of preposition: James had to be punished for lying.

Gerunds do not always stand alone as a single noun but can be part of a phrase. Because the gerund is derived from a verb, it can be the introductory element of a complete sentence, in which it replaces the subject and verb of the sentence. Consider how the initial sentence below is changed *to become* a gerund followed by the elements of the initial sentence:

John watches a baseball game. (*John* = subject; *watches* = verb)
Watching a baseball game is always fun. (*watching* = subject)
Bill never liked watching a baseball game. (*watching* = direct object)
A good time is watching a baseball game. (*watching* = subject complement)
Are you interested in watching a baseball game? (*watching* = object of preposition)

This concept of replacing a subject and verb with a gerund is widely used, and it explains why a gerund can be followed by a direct object, indirect object, object of a preposition, or an adverb. For example:

Tina buys **a new car**. (direct object)
I have no interest in buying a new car.

George gives **her a ring**. (indirect object and direct object)
Giving her a ring will make her very happy.

We speak **angrily with the clerk**. (adverb and prepositional phrase)
Speaking angrily with the clerk doesn't solve the problem.

Since gerunds are nouns, they can be modified by possessive adjectives:

Her swimming breaks all records.
Mr. Garcia doesn't care for my singing.
Do you like their dancing?
His strongest event is his tumbling.

It is possible to use other adjectives as the modifiers of gerunds, but that function has to be used with care, because some adjectives sound awkward with gerunds. The following sentences illustrate the appropriate use of adjectives with gerunds:

Regular dating means developing a relationship.
The coach demands **rigorous** training for the team.

Infinitives

Infinitives are *verbals* that function as nouns. They are formed from the base form of the verb that is preceded by the particle word *to*: *to have*, *to help*, *to see*, and so on. Since the function of this type of verb is to act as a noun, it can be the subject, the direct object, the subject complement, and even the adverb in a sentence. Compare infinitives used as subjects and standard nouns used as subjects. Infinitives are never preceded by a definite or indefinite article (*the, a, an*):

Infinitive	Noun
To laugh makes me happy.	A good book makes me happy.
To argue helps no one.	His attitude helps no one.

Compare infinitives and nouns used as a direct object:

Infinitive	Noun
I hate to complain.	I hate broccoli.
You don't need to worry.	You don't need a new bike.

Compare infinitives and nouns used as subject complements:

Infinitive	Noun
My goal is to paint.	My goal is a good job.
Her only wish was to dance.	Her only wish was peace.

Compare infinitives used adverbially and standard adverbs:

Infinitive	Adverb
Bill needs to practice to win.	Bill needs to practice regularly.
We had to study to learn.	We had to study hard.

Like gerunds, infinitives can be part of a longer phrase:

To participate in sports requires good grades.
I really wanted **to sing in our university choir.**
My only wish was **to help her and her family.**

Like gerunds, infinitives can be the replacement of the subject and verb of a complete sentence:

Mark developed a new medicine. (*Mark* = subject; *developed* = verb)
To develop a new medicine is not an easy process. (*to develop* = subject)
The scientists tried to develop a new medicine. (*to develop* = direct object)

Everyone took part in the play. (*everyone* = subject; *took part* = verb)
To take part in the play required some courage. (*to take part* = subject)
Linda doesn't want to take part in the play. (*to take part* = direct object)

Many transitive verbs can be followed by infinitive phrases. Some of the most commonly used are:

agree	fail	learn	prefer	remember
begin	hesitate	neglect	pretend	start
continue	hope	offer	promise	try
decide	intend	plan	refuse	

Consider these example sentences:

They haven't decided **to sell them the latest computers.**
I hope **to borrow enough money** so I can buy a house.
The girls pretended **not to see the boys.**
You just can't refuse **to help these unfortunate people out.**

Sometimes a noun or pronoun can be placed before an infinitive phrase. It functions as the *direct object of the transitive verb* in the sentence but provides the meaning of the subject of the sentence from which the infinitive phrase has been derived. For example:

He finds a room for the party.
John asks **him** to find a room for the party.

The men play cards in the living room.
She didn't want **the men** to play cards in the living room.

There are several transitive verbs that can be followed by a *direct object* and infinitive phrase:

advise	force	remind
allow	hire	teach
appoint	invite	tell
convince	order	
encourage	permit	

Consider these example sentences:

They advised **her to remain at home until further notice.**
The professor taught **his students to think independently.**
Why didn't you tell **me to phone Mr. Bennett?**
The manager invited **us to meet with her in her office.**

8. Reflexive Verbs

Reflexive Pronouns

The reflexive pronouns are the reflexive counterparts of personal pronouns. Consider the following pairs of pronouns:

Personal Pronoun	Reflexive Pronoun
I	myself
you (*sing.*)	yourself
he	himself
she	herself
it	itself
one	oneself
we	ourselves
you (*pl.*)	yourselves
they	themselves

There are only a few verbs in English that are true reflexive verbs (the combination of a verb and a reflexive pronoun). A true reflexive verb is one that must be used together with a reflexive pronoun to have meaning. The verb cannot be used with a noun or pronoun object other than the reflexive pronoun. For example:

I perjure myself	we perjure ourselves
you perjure yourself	you perjure yourselves
he perjures himself	they perjure themselves
she perjures herself	
one perjures oneself	

Other true reflexive verbs are *absent oneself* and *bestir oneself*. These verbs are always used with a reflexive pronoun.

Other verbs that are not true reflexive verbs can be used with reflexive pronouns as a replacement for a direct or indirect object noun or pronoun.

Similar to true reflexive verbs, these verbs do not have complete meaning unless they are followed by a direct object or a reflexive pronoun:

I enjoyed the party.	I enjoyed myself. (direct object)
She considered him lucky.	She considered herself lucky.
	(direct object)

You cannot merely say, "I enjoyed" or "She considered lucky." An object or reflexive pronoun is required with such verbs.

See Chapter 13 for details on reflexive pronouns.

9. The Passive Voice

The passive voice is formed with the auxiliary *to be* and a past participle of either a regular or an irregular verb. However, the participle can only be formed from a transitive verb. For example:

to fire	The new salesman is fired.
to break	The large window was broken during a storm.
to find	The children were found by a kind old man.

The auxiliary *to be* can be conjugated in any tense:

Present: She is hired for the job.
Past: She was hired for the job.
Present perfect: She has been hired for the job.
Past perfect: She had been hired for the job.
Future: She will be hired for the job.
Future perfect: She will have been hired for the job.

The Active Voice

A sentence in the active voice that has a transitive verb can be changed to the passive voice. But the function of the elements of the active sentence are different from their function in the passive sentence. Consider how the following active sentence changes to a passive sentence:

Active: John developed a new plan for the project.
Passive: A new plan for the project was developed by John.

1. The active subject becomes the object of the preposition *by: by John.*

2. The transitive verb in the active sentence is formed as a participle: *developed.*

3. The tense of the transitive verb in the active sentence (*developed* = past tense) becomes the tense of the auxiliary *to be: was.*

4. The object of the active sentence becomes the subject of the passive sentence: *a new plan for the project.*

This process is used to change other active sentences to the passive voice:

Active Sentence	Passive Sentence
Tom will deliver the message.	The message will be delivered by Tom.
Everyone has taken the oath.	The oath has been taken by everyone.
He punished the boy.	The boy was punished by him.

When a writer or speaker wishes to make the doer of an action *anonymous*, he or she can change an active sentence to the passive and omit the prepositional phrase that is introduced by the preposition *by*:

Active Sentence	Passive Sentence
The mayor began the project.	The project was begun by the mayor.
	The project was begun. (anonymous doer)
A blizzard buried the car in the snow.	The car was buried in the snow by a blizzard.
	The car was buried in the snow. (anonymous doer)

If the doer of the action of an active sentence is a vague pronoun or noun, the doer of the action can be omitted from the passive form of the sentence. Some vague entities are *one*, *some*, *they*, and *people*:

Active Sentence	Passive Sentence
One needs money to travel.	Money is needed to travel.
They grow rice in this region.	Rice is grown in this region.
People admire him greatly.	He is admired greatly.

Writers or speakers may wish to conceal the source of their information or make a generalization. In such cases, the impersonal pronoun *it* becomes the subject of a passive-voice phrase that introduces another clause. For example:

It has been stated that this company will not survive another month.
It is sometimes said that money cannot buy happiness.
At that time **it was commonly believed** that the earth was flat.

Progressive Formation

The progressive conjugation of the passive auxiliary *to be* indicates that the action of the passive verb is in progress, incomplete, or interrupted, just as it does with active verbs. Compare the following sentences:

Complete: Mary was taken to the hospital. (Mary arrived at the hospital.)
Progressive: Mary was being taken to the hospital. (Mary's arrival is not certain.)

Complete: I was warned by my boss. (My boss's warning is over.)
Progressive: I was being warned by my boss. (My boss's warning was continuing.)

Note that the progressive forms of *to be* appear primarily in the present and past tenses. In other tenses, they sound awkward and should be avoided:

Mary is being taken to the hospital.
Mary was being taken to the hospital.

I am being warned by my boss.
I was being warned by my boss.

Auxiliaries

Any variety of auxiliaries can be used together with the passive voice. But when there is another auxiliary in the sentence, the passive auxiliary *to be* is always in infinitive form. There is no change to the past participle. Since some auxiliaries are followed by the full infinitive and others omit the particle word *to* from the infinitive, it is important to identify which kind of auxiliary is being used. Let's review some commonly used auxiliaries:

Full Infinitive Follows	**Particle Word *to* Is Omitted**
to have to	must
to be able to	can
to want to	should
to like to	would

Compare the following two groups of passive sentences. Note how the auxiliary *to be* differs in each group:

The text has to be corrected again.
She won't be able to be interviewed today.
Young William has never wanted to be made king.
These scales must be practiced every day.
His poems can be understood by any average person.
If I had the right tools, the repair would be completed today.

Questions in the Passive Voice

When asking a question in the passive voice, the auxiliary verb precedes the subject of the sentence in all tenses:

Are you being treated well?
Was the addition to the school eventually built?
Have the men been instructed in the use of this machine?
Had he been cared for by the nursing staff?
Will the mortgage be paid off?

If other auxiliaries are used together with *to be* and a past participle, the kind of auxiliary and the tense determine whether a form of *to do* is needed to ask a question. With the auxiliaries *to have to*, *to want to*, and *to like to*, a form of *to do* is used to ask a question in the present and past tenses. With *can*, *could*, *should*, and *would* as well as with other auxiliaries that begin with *to be* (*to be able to*, *to be supposed to*), a form of *to do* is not needed. Compare these two groups of sentences:

Present	Do they have to be finished by tomorrow?
Past	Did Tina want to be promoted to manager?
Present Perfect	Have you really had to be helped with this easy task?
Future	Will Ms. Marsh want to be picked up by 9 A.M. again?

Present	Can our group be guided by that nice, young man over there?
Past	Could the text be translated into English by 3 P.M.?
Present Perfect	Have they been able to be treated by Dr. Phillips?
Future	Will the patients be able to be removed safely during an emergency?

Note that *to be supposed to* can sound awkward in the perfect and future tenses and should be avoided.

Stative Passive

Another form of the passive is known as the *stative passive*. It is structurally the same as the passive described previously. However, the meaning of a sentence in the stative passive is different: *The past participle is considered a modifier* and is used much like any other adjective in a predicate following the verb *to be*. For example:

The clock is broken and useless to me.

In this sentence the participle *broken* is a modifier; and the adjective *useless* is also a modifier. Both words modify *clock*. Let's look at another example:

The man was frightened but happy to be alive.

In this example, *man* is modified by the participle *frightened* and the adjective *happy*.

The passive voice and the stative passive are not always clearly differentiated. However, if the sentence has a prepositional phrase introduced by the preposition *by*, it indicates that there is a *doer* of the action described by the participle, and, therefore, the sentence is not in the stative passive:

Passive Voice or Stative Passive	Passive Voice
The fields **were drained**.	The fields **were drained** by the farmers.
The toy **is repaired**.	The toy **is repaired** by Mr. Johnson.
Several soldiers **were wounded**.	Several soldiers **were wounded** by shrapnel.

It is often the intent of the writer or speaker that determines whether a participle should be understood as a verb in the passive voice or as a modifier in the stative passive.

Differentiating the two forms is easier when the passive auxiliary *to be* is in its progressive form:

The fields were being drained. (This was an action in the past; it is the passive voice.)
The toy is being repaired now. (This is an action in the present; it is the passive voice.)

The addition of other auxiliaries does not make the difference between the passive voice and the stative passive much clearer. It is still a matter of intent, but the tendency is to regard passive sentences with auxiliaries to be in the passive voice:

She could not be promoted to manager without developing further skills.
I want to be informed of every problem that takes place.
You have to be treated by a specialist.

10. The Subjunctive Mood

The English subjunctive occurs in two forms: the present subjunctive and the past subjunctive. The present subjunctive is derived from the infinitive of a verb and is in the same form for all persons. No distinctions are made between regular and irregular verbs. For example:

	to be	*to have*	*to go*	*to see*	*to like*
I	be	have	go	see	like
you (*sing.*)	be	have	go	see	like
he/she/it	be	have	go	see	like
we	be	have	go	see	like
you (*pl.*)	be	have	go	sec	like
they	be	have	go	see	like

The past subjunctive is derived from the past tense of a verb. In the case of the verb *to be*, only the plural form (*were*) is used in the past subjunctive:

	to be	*to have*	*to go*	*to see*	*to like*
I	were	had	went	saw	liked
you (*sing.*)	were	had	went	saw	liked
he/she/it	were	had	went	saw	liked
we	were	had	went	saw	liked
you (*pl.*)	were	had	went	saw	liked
they	were	had	went	saw	liked

Another form of the past subjunctive is the combination of the auxiliary *would* and an infinitive:

	to be	*to go*	*to like*
I	would be	would go	would like
you (*sing.*)	would be	would go	would like
he/she/it	would be	would go	would like
we	would be	would go	would like
you (*pl.*)	would be	would go	would like
they	would be	would go	would like

Use of the Present Subjunctive

The present subjunctive is used in a clause that follows a phrase that states that something is *necessary* or *important*:

It is necessary that Ms. Wade **be** transferred to another department.
We regard it as important that he **have** full access to the documents.

Other statements that are similar in meaning to those illustrated above can also introduce a present subjunctive clause, such as:

It is imperative.	It is vital.	I believe it is urgent.
We consider it a necessity.	It is crucial.	It is essential.

The present subjunctive is also used to describe the action of a verb in a clause that follows statements that contain the verbs *ask, command, demand, insist, propose, recommend, request,* and *suggest*:

My lawyer asked that juror two **be** excused.
I insisted that Mr. Drake **come** to the meeting on time today.
No one suggested that she **move** out of the apartment tomorrow.

Notice that the present subjunctive infers that the action of the verb in these sentences is taking place in either the present or the future:

The king commanded that his warriors **be** ready for war **today**.
I recommend you **borrow** the money sometime **next month**.

The conjunction *that*, which combines the introductory clause with the present subjunctive clause, is usually optional:

John made the request that his idea be discussed thoroughly.
John made the request his idea be discussed thoroughly.

Using the Past Subjunctive

The verb that follows a *wish* clause is expressed in the past subjunctive. However, the meaning is inferred to be in the present tense. The conjunction *that* is optional in combining a *wish* clause with a past subjunctive clause:

I wish my son were back from Afghanistan. (now, in the present)
Mother wishes that Tina came by for dinner more often. (now, in the present)

If the verb *wish* is in a form of the past tense, the past subjunctive verb suggests the past tense:

Mother wished that Tina came by for dinner more often. (in the past)
I had always wished you knew how much I loved you. (in the past)

Use the past subjunctive in clauses that are introduced by *if* and *as if.* If a single verb is used in the non-*if* clause, the past subjunctive *would* is used with the accompanying verb in infinitive form:

If Mary studied more, she would be a great scholar.
I wouldn't be so confident if I were you.
My brother acted as if he played basketball like a superstar.
The visiting prince spoke as if he were one of the common people.

When you form an imperative sentence with *suppose*, the statement that follows is in the past subjunctive with *would* plus an infinitive:

Suppose your mother saw you right now. You would be very
    embarrassed.
Suppose Tom asked you to the dance. Would you really go out with
    him?

A verb conjugated in a perfect tense (*have* + past participle) suggests that the action of the verb is in the past tense:

Laura wishes she had been invited to the wedding. (Invitations were
    sent in the past.)
He wished he had had better luck in Las Vegas. (He visited Las Vegas
    in the past.)

This occurs with *if* clauses as well:

If only there had been a way to help her.
If I had seen the pickpocket, I would have reported him to the police.
Jim would have changed the tire if he had had a jack.

Note that *would* is still used in the non-*if* clause when the verb is in a present perfect-tense form (*would have changed*).

If clauses are used to set a *condition*. The accompanying clause states the result that would occur if the condition were met. For example:

Condition	Result
If Jean were here,	she would know what to do.
If Jean had been here,	she would have known what to do.

This use of *would* in a clause that states a result is also used when other auxiliaries are added to the clause. For example:

If Jean **had to** work this evening, she would **have to** miss the party.
If you really **wanted to** be a pianist, you would **want to** practice more.

The inference of the present or the past tense occurs respectively when you use *would* plus an infinitive for the present and *would* plus *have* plus a past participle for the past.

If you spoke German, you would **be able to** understand Grandfather.
If you had learned German, you would **have been able to** understand
 Grandfather.

When the auxiliary *can* is used in the clause that sets the condition, the auxiliary is in the past subjunctive (*could*). The accompanying verb is in its infinitive form for the present-tense meaning or formed as *have* plus a past participle for the past-tense meaning. If the clause that states the result contains the auxiliary *could*, *would* is not used. Let's look at some examples:

If Bill **could** speak French, he would visit Paris.
If Bill spoke French, he **could** visit Paris.

If Mr. Brown **could** have remembered what time the train departed, he
 wouldn't have missed it.
If Mr. Brown had remembered what time the train departed, he **could**
 have taken it home.

When *have* and a past participle follow certain auxiliaries in the past subjunctive, a special meaning is derived. This structure suggests that the action of the verb is *imaginary, a desired outcome,* or merely *a possibility.* These auxiliaries are *could have, might have, must have, ought to have,* and *should have.* Let's look at some example sentences:

I could have been a famous astronaut. (imaginary)
Jim might have become a dentist. (a possibility)
Dad must have missed the train again. (a possibility)
You ought to have followed the directions. (desired outcome)
Martin should have married Barbara instead. (desired outcome)

In many cases, the same phrase can be used with any of the auxiliaries:

It could have been a wonderful vacation.
It might have been a wonderful vacation.
It ought to have been a wonderful vacation.
It must have been a wonderful vacation.
It should have been a wonderful vacation.

He could have been an opera singer.
He might have been an opera singer.
He ought to have been an opera singer.
He must have been an opera singer.
He should have been an opera singer.

11. Phrasal Verbs

Phrasal verbs are composed of a verb plus adverbs and/or prepositions. The prepositions in phrasal verbs are often used as adverbs. What is important about phrasal verbs is that well-known verbs no longer mean what they normally do when they function as phrasal verbs. It is the combination of verb + adverb + preposition that derives a completely and often radically different meaning from the individual verb. For example:

Individual Verb	Phrasal Verb and New Meaning
to set (to place)	*to set out for* (to begin a journey to)
to come (to arrive)	*to come to* (to regain consciousness)
to bring (to convey, fetch)	*to bring up* (to educate; to introduce)

Phrasal verbs are used in all tenses, voices, and moods just like any other verbs. Let's look at some sentences with the verb *to bring up* (to introduce), used in a variety of ways:

Why are you bringing that up again?
I never should have brought his money problems up.
The changes to the plans were brought up during the last meeting.
Don't bring up the recent losses in the stock market.

The list of English phrasal verbs is very long. It is wise to use a dictionary of phrasal verbs when using this unique verb form in order to have the precise meaning of each phrasal verb. A sampling of phrasal verbs and their usage will be given here:

Phrasal Verbs Derived from *to be*

to be on	(an apparatus or machinery is functioning; the opposite of *to be off*)
	Is the washing machine still on? No, it's off.
to be with it	(to be contemporary or in fashion)
	Her hairdo is old-fashioned. Why can't she be more with it?
to be up to something	(to look suspicious; sometimes stated as *to be up to no good*)
	Is that man over there up to something? He looks like he's up to no good.

Phrasal Verb Derived from *to catch*

to catch on   (to suddenly understand a situation or a joke)
                     I suddenly caught on and knew I was the subject of
                     their conversation.

Phrasal Verbs Derived from *to do*

to do over   (to perform again or bring about again)
                     That's wrong. Do that problem over.
                     (to redecorate or to improve someone's appearance)
                     Jean wants to do over her bedroom.
                     With a little makeup, I can do you over completely.
to do with   (to deal with or endure someone or something)
                     I can't do with this old car anymore. I need a new one.

Phrasal Verbs Derived from *to drop*

to drop off   (to fall asleep or to fall off something)
                     Little Bobby was tired and quickly dropped off.
                     A large bank of snow dropped off the roof.
to drop off at   (to deliver someone or something to a certain
                     location)
                     Mr. Johnson dropped the laundry off at the cleaners.

Phrasal Verbs Derived from *to get*

to get back   (to return from someplace)
                     When did your brother get back from Afghanistan?
to get back at   (to seek revenge upon someone)
                     She said she'd get back at you for lying about her.
to get behind   (to support or promote someone or some activity)
                     We have to get behind our candidate if we want her
                     to win.
to get behind in   (to be late or to lag behind in performing a task)
                     This department is getting behind in its work again.
to get in on   (to become part of a financial arrangement or to
                     participate in an event)
                     We got in on a deal to sell electronics in Russia.
                     You have to pay a registration fee if you want to get
                     in on the conference.
to get into it   (to have an argument or a fight about something)
  (over)   My in-laws always got into it over money.

Phrasal Verbs Derived from *to keep*

to keep up   (to hold someone or something upright or to prevent
                     someone from falling asleep)
                     She's fainting! Keep her up! Don't let her fall!

	Somehow we kept the boy up until his parents arrived.
to keep up with	(to maintain the same speed with someone or something)
	Run a little slower. I just can't keep up with you.
to lay off (of)	(to stop harassing or bothering someone; the preposition *of* is optional)
	Mary just wouldn't lay off (of) the man who dented her new car.
to lay off (from)	(to end someone's employment)
	They plan to lay off our entire department.
	John was laid off from a job he'd had for ten years.

Phrasal Verbs Derived from *to make*

to make of	(to interpret someone or something)
	What do you make of this message from the manager?
to make some-thing of	(to become a success)
	Karen has made something of herself and is worth a lot of money.
to make out	(to begin to see clearly)
	In this fog it's hard to make out the skyline of San Francisco.
to make out of	(to create an image of someone or something that is different from the real one)
	Don't make a big problem out of a very simple matter.
to make up	(to fabricate stories about a person or to put cosmetics on a person)
	Why did you make up those stories about me?
	Laura wanted to make up her face and comb her hair.
to make it up to	(to compensate a person for something)
	I want to make it up to you for having scratched your new piano.
to make up with	(to reconcile with a person)
	Despite their argument, Mary wanted to make up with Jim.

Phrasal Verbs Derived from *to put*

to put down (for)	(to demean or ridicule a person [for doing something])
	He tries so hard, but still you put him down.
	Bill's not good at tennis, but we can't put him down for trying.

to put on   (to wear headgear or a garment, to pretend, or to tease)

Tom put on a hat and a new suit and went to the meeting.

She's not really sleeping. She's just putting on.

Jane is pregnant again? Really? You're putting me on!

to put up with   (to endure or bear something unpleasant)

I can't put up with your lying anymore.

Phrasal Verbs Derived from *to stand*

to stand for   (to be the symbol for something or to tolerate something)

The American flag stands for freedom and democracy.

Mom would never stand for our using bad language.

to stand in (for)   (to be a substitute for someone)

Jim will stand in for the manager while she's in New York.

Phrasal Verbs Derived from *to take*

to take back   (to return something or to remind someone of a time in the past)

Did you take the lawn mower back to Mr. Simms?

Hearing that song again took me back to when I was in school.

to take back from   (to return something to the original owner from someone)

Bill wants to take back the diamond earrings from me.

to take down   (to write something on paper or to raze or dismantle something)

She took down my phone number and promised to call.

The city plans on taking down the old library building.

to take down from   (to remove something or someone from a high location)

Can you help me take that box down from the shelf?

to take in   (to decrease the size of a garment, to provide someone with shelter, or to deceive someone)

You've lost some weight. You should take those
pants in.

We took a homeless man in for a night.

Alex took me in with one of his schemes again.

Phrasal Verbs Derived from *to walk*

to walk out on   (to jilt or abandon someone)
I can't believe that my wife walked out on me.

to walk up to   (to approach someone or something)
She walked up to Bob and slapped him in the face.

Phrasal Verbs Derived from *to warm*

to warm up   (to grow warm)
It'll start to warm up again in May.

to warm up to   (to feel comfortable with a person or about a thing)
Mary quickly warmed up to the charming man.

Phrasal Verbs Derived from *to wash*

to wash out   (to give something a light wash or to exhaust or
weaken someone)
I need to wash out a pair of socks.
A whole day of hiking has really washed me out.

to wash out of   (to fail at an activity and be required to leave)
Bill tried hard, but he eventually washed out of
the military academy.

Phrasal Verbs Derived from *to work*

to work out   (to do physical exercise or to end satisfactorily)
I used to work out at this gym.
They tried living together, but it just didn't
work out.

to work up   (to prepare something or to be upset or in an
emotional state)
The manager worked up a new sales program.
Mary was all worked up and began to cry.

to work up to   (to find a way to say or do something)
The angry workers are working up to a strike.

Phrasal Verbs Derived from *to write*

to write off   (to deduct something from one's taxes or to give
up hope on someone)
We can write off some of these repairs on our tax
return.
He began to drink a lot, and his friends soon wrote
him off.

to write off for	(to contact a company in order to purchase something through the mail)
	I filled out the discount coupon and wrote off for the video camera.
to write out	(to write something completely or to put something in writing)
	Write the essay out with the appropriate margins.
	I wrote the directions out for you so you won't get lost.

Placement of the Preposition Used as an Adverb

Some adverbs in phrasal verbs can be placed in two different positions in a sentence. If the object in the sentence is a noun, the adverb can be placed either before the object or after the object. However, if the object is a pronoun, the adverb can only follow the object. For example:

Why did you bring **up** that issue?
Why did you bring that issue **up**?
Why did you bring it **up**?

Mr. Edwards dropped **off** the children at school.
Mr. Edwards dropped the children **off** at school.
Mr. Edwards dropped them **off** at school.

John took **back** his ring.
John took his ring **back**.
John took it **back**.

If the adverb in a phrasal verb precedes a prepositional phrase, the adverb has only one position in the sentence: immediately in front of the prepositional phrase:

We usually work out **at this gym**.
We kept the boy up **until his parents arrived**.
Write the essay out **with the appropriate margins**.

Part 2

Essentials of Grammar

12. Definite and Indefinite Articles

Most English nouns are preceded by either a definite article (*the*) or an indefinite article (*a, an*). In some languages, the definite article helps to identify the *gender* (masculine, feminine, or neuter) of a noun or to show the difference between a singular and a plural noun. But the English definite article is used with any gender and can be singular or plural:

	Singular	**Plural**
Masculine	the boy	the boys
Feminine	the aunt	the aunts
Neuter	the rock	the rocks

Although the definite articles shown look identical, they are not always pronounced in the same way. If a noun begins with a consonant, the letter *e* in *the* is pronounced like a *schwa* sound. That is, it sounds like *uh*: *thuh*. The *schwa* sound is often represented by an upside-down *e*: ə.

When the definite article precedes a word that begins with a vowel, the definite article is pronounced as *thee*. For example:

	Singular	**Plural**
Masculine	thə boy	thə boys
Feminine	thee aunt	thee aunts
Neuter	thə rock	thə rocks

The indefinite articles *a* and *an* are used respectively to precede a word that begins with a consonant and a word that begins with a vowel. An indefinite or unspecific meaning is derived in the plural by using no article at all:

	Singular	**Plural**
Masculine	a man	men
Feminine	an actress	actresses
Neuter	a use	uses

Note: When the vowel sound *u* is pronounced as *uh*, it is preceded by *an* (an uncle). When the vowel sound *u* is pronounced as *yoo*, it is preceded by *a* (a university, a European).

Except when a speaker wishes to be emphatic, the article *a* is pronounced like ə (*uh*):

	Singular	**Plural**
Masculine	ə man	men
Feminine	an actress	actresses
Neuter	ə use	uses

Articles do not always precede a noun. They can precede adverbs or adjectives as well. Therefore, it is not the first letter of a noun that determines the use and pronunciation of *the*, *a*, or *an*, but the word that stands directly behind the article. For example:

the answer (pronounced *thee*)
the written answer (pronounced *thə*)
the correctly written answer (pronounced *thə*)
an orchard (pronounced *an*)
a dying orchard (pronounced ə)
a slowly dying orchard (pronounced ə)

Using Definite Articles

Definite articles identify a specific person or thing in a group. They are used with either singular or plural nouns and refer to a person or thing that has been previously mentioned. The previously mentioned person or thing is initially identified with *a* or *an*, but once it has been brought up, it is now specific and uses *the*. Let's look at some examples:

A strange man was standing on the corner. No one had ever seen **the** man before.
Jim is carrying **a** box. I'm curious to know what's in **the** box.
Did you get **a** gift from Aunt Mary? Yes, **the** gift arrived today by UPS.

If the two speakers have previously talked about something, both the question and answer will use definite articles:

Where's **the** new flashlight? I haven't seen **the** flashlight since you brought it home.
Did you empty **the** dishwasher? I haven't even run **the** dishwasher yet.

A definite article should also be used with the following:

1. Bodies of water (the Mississippi, the Atlantic, the Red Sea)

2. Geographical regions (the Middle East, the Old South, the Far East)

3. Deserts, mountain ranges, and peninsulas (the Sahara, the Rocky Mountains, the Florida peninsula)

4. Specific points on the globe (the South Pole, the Equator, the Prime Meridian)

5. Island chains (the Aleutians, the Hebrides, the Canary Islands)

6. Superlatives (the oldest, the best one, the tallest)

7. Ordinal numbers (the first, the ninth floor, the Sixteenth Amendment)

8. Unique things and places (the White House, the moon, the sun)

9. Decades (the fifties, the eighties, the nineties)

10. To identify a specific person or thing (the woman who won the prize, the books that were stolen, the house on Elm Street)

Note that country names that are plural require the use of the definite article: the United States of America, the Netherlands.

Some English nouns are called non-count nouns. They identify something in general or something that cannot be counted. If the noun is something in general, the definite article is not used:

I find **spelling** rather difficult.
She likes classical **music**.
Ignorance is no excuse for breaking the law.

The definite article can be used with these generalities to make them specific:

The spelling in your essay was horrible.
I really liked **the music** that Bob was playing.
The ignorance of that man is not to be believed!

Other non-count nouns refer to things that cannot be counted (sugar, coffee, work, and so on). The definite article is not used with this category of nouns when they are treated as generalities:

Rice is the staple food in much of Asia.
Is **tea** still the preferred beverage in England?
A lot of **lumber** is needed for this construction project.

The use of the definite article with non-count nouns makes them specific:

The rice in that bowl looks bad.
I don't like **the** strong **tea** that Aunt Louise serves.
When will you deliver **the lumber** for this project?

Using Indefinite Articles

Indefinite articles are used when the noun they modify is not specific. No particular person or thing is being identified. If the noun is plural, no article is used with it. Although *any* or *some* often accompany a plural noun, the meaning is still not specific:

Singular: A map is required if you plan to hike in these mountains.
Plural: Maps don't always help if you get lost in these mountains.

Singular: Do you have **an** orange?
Plural: Do you have **any** oranges?

Singular: A soldier was wounded in the battle.
Plural: Some soldiers were wounded in the battle.

A negative answer to a question that inquires about an unspecified person or thing will use the indefinite article in the answer. Compare these answers to the positive answers provided in the preceding section, "Using Definite Articles:"

Did you get **a** gift from her? No, I still haven't received **a** gift from her.
Was **a** child involved in the accident? No, the report didn't mention **a** child.
Did you get your medicine at **a** drugstore? No, I couldn't find **a** drugstore that was open.

Indefinite articles should be used with the following:

1. Professions (a teacher, a lawyer, an astronaut)

2. Nationalities (a Russian, a Mexican, an Iranian)

3. Religions (a Jew, a Christian, a Buddhist)

4. Following *there is* or *there are* (There is a reason for it. There are some problems with it.)

5. Unspecified nouns that can be counted (a book, an orange, some trees)

6. Names of days (on a Monday; it was a Friday; on a Saturday)

7. With certain numbers (a hundred, a thousand, a billion)

When Articles Are Not Required

Neither a definite article nor an indefinite article should be used with the following:

1. Street names (Pennsylvania Avenue, State Street, Interstate 90)

2. City names and states (Madrid, Berlin, California)

3. Continents and country names that are singular (Africa, Germany, France)

4. Lakes and mountains (Lake Michigan, Lake Constance, Mount Everest)

5. Islands (Madagascar, Easter Island, Oahu)

6. Academic subjects (history, mathematics, home economics)

7. Sports (baseball, tennis, rugby)

8. Languages and nationalities (Canadian, Italian, Korean)

9. Mealtimes (breakfast, lunch, dinner)

10. Years (in 54 B.C., before 350 A.D., in 2010)

11. Professions (law, engineering, teaching)

12. Stores and businesses (Macy's, Home Depot, Bank of America)

13. Transportation (by car, by train, by bus)

14. Regularly attended places (in bed, at school, in jail)

Contrasting General and Specific Meaning

In many sentences, either the definite article or the indefinite article can be used. Of course, there is a difference in meaning. Let's look at some pairs of sentences and how they differ, depending upon the article used:

A bear roamed through the campground. (No one had seen this bear before.)
The bear roamed through the campground. (It was the same bear I saw in the forest.)

Do you have a passport? (I'm inquiring for the first time about this.)
Do you have the passport? (I gave you mine for safekeeping earlier.)

Sharks like to feed on seals. (a statement about any sharks)
The sharks like to feed on seals. (These are the sharks we see from our boat.)

The existence of definite and indefinite articles in English is an essential part of how the language distinguishes a thing or things in general and the previously mentioned thing or things specifically. Use these articles carefully and with the awareness of the distinctions you can make by their use.

13. Nouns and Pronouns

Nouns

Nouns are words that describe a living thing, a place, an object, or a concept. For example:

The president was elected in a landslide. (living thing)
We lived in **Cleveland** for ten years. (place)
Did you sell **the painting** of Uncle Ben? (object)
Freedom must be protected. (concept)

Because English has so few signals, such as endings that identify a word as a particular part of speech, it is sometimes difficult to determine whether a word is a noun or another part of speech. Consider the following groups of sentences and how the same word functions as a different part of speech:

We need more **feed** for the cattle. (noun)
Feed the dogs when you get home tonight. (verb)
I had to put in a new **feed** pipe to the furnace. (adjective)

The **fish** in this lake are not edible. (noun)
You shouldn't **fish** without a license. (verb)
The **fish** warden fined him for catching more than the limit. (adjective)

A lot of **steel** will be needed for this project. (noun)
He needs to **steel** himself against the pain. (verb)
The engraving was put on a **steel** plate. (adjective)

A noun has to be identified by its use in a sentence. If a word is functioning in one of the following ways, it is a noun:

1. The subject of a sentence (**The boy** lived nearby.)

2. The direct object of a sentence (We saw **the boy** at the river.)

3. The indirect object of a sentence (I gave **the boy** a sandwich.)

4. An appositive (A handsome lad, **a boy** of about twelve, approached us.)

5. The object of a preposition (She tried to speak with **the boy**.)

There are many different kinds of nouns in English, such as common nouns, proper nouns, countable nouns, non-count nouns, collective nouns, concrete nouns, and abstract nouns.

Common Nouns

Common nouns describe ordinary people and things or people and things in general. For example:

cat	house	school
drum	junk	tree
flag	kitchen	vines
garage	mountain	zoo

Proper Nouns

Proper nouns refer to nouns that identify the specific name that describes someone or some product, company, or institution. For example:

Dr. Jones	Microsoft	Sears Roebuck
Jean Keller	the *Wall Street Journal*	Tiny Tim
Mr. Jackson	Boeing Aircraft	the White House

Countable Nouns

Countable nouns are precisely those nouns that describe things that can be counted. Countable nouns have a plural form. For example:

book(s)	match(es)	sock(s)
car(s)	needle(s)	tool(s)
goose (geese)	pen(s)	wig(s)

Non-Count Nouns

Non-count nouns are nouns that are in a particular kind of state that cannot be counted:

air	gasoline	smoke
dust	light	sunshine
fire	oxygen	water

This category of nouns can be identified by attempting to count them. You then discover that you cannot have *five dusts, six oxygens*, or *eleven sunshines*.

Collective Nouns

Collective nouns describe a group of people or things. Most collective nouns can be both singular and plural:

band(s) of thieves	herd(s) of elephant	swarm(s) of bees
class(es)	pack(s) of dogs	team(s)
family (families)	police	union(s)

Concrete Nouns

Concrete nouns are words that have a physical shape that can be seen or touched. They can come from other categories of nouns:

animal	magazine	shoe
child	plank	teapot
horse	rope	vase

Abstract Nouns

Abstract nouns differ from concrete nouns in that they do not have a physical shape. They describe ideas, qualities, or feelings:

anger	ignorance	love
bravery	intelligence	peace
hate	knowledge	sympathy

Pronouns

There is more than one type of pronoun. The most commonly used pronouns are personal pronouns, which have four forms: the subjective form, used when a pronoun is the subject of a sentence; the objective form, used when a pronoun is a direct or indirect object or the object of a preposition; and two possessive forms. (Note that possessives will be taken up in detail in Chapter 23.)

	Subjective	Objective	Possessive
First-person singular	I	me	my/mine
Second-person singular	you (*sing.*)	you	your/yours
Third-person singular	he	him	his/his
Third-person singular	she	her	her/hers
Third-person singular	it	it	its/its
First-person plural	we	us	our/ours
Second-person plural	you (*pl.*)	you	your/yours
Third-person plural	they	them	their/theirs

Let's look at how some of these pronouns are used in sentences:

I just joined the new chess club. (subject)
The boys will help **you** with the gardening. (direct object)
Who gave **him** all that money? (indirect object)
Jim danced with **her** all night long. (object of preposition)
Our daughter is going to her first prom. (possessive)
Is **yours** a good dancer, too? (possessive)

Only the third-person singular and plural pronouns can replace nouns in a sentence. A form of *he* replaces masculine nouns; a form of *she* replaces feminine nouns; a form of *it* replaces neuter nouns; and a form of *they* replaces all plural nouns:

The young actor suddenly forgot his lines. **He** suddenly forgot his lines.
Have you met **Ms. Brown**? Have you met **her**?
I was never interested in **science**. I was never interested in **it**.
The mountains' ravines were hidden beneath the snow. **Their** ravines were hidden beneath the snow.

There are a few instances when an inanimate object is referred to as a *feminine* noun rather than as a *neuter* noun. This occurs with ships and with other objects, for which a person might feel a certain amount of affection:

The M.S. *Morrow* stood at dock. **She** would sail in the morning on the tide.
I've had **that old Ford** for twelve years. **She**'s a great old car.

The third-person-singular pronoun *one* generally means *someone* and is used formally in place of the less formal *you*. For example:

- *You* meaning *someone*:

  You have to be on your guard when you're dealing with that gang of ruffians. They'll beat you up and take your money. You need to be smart and keep your distance.

- *One* meaning *someone*:

  One has to be on one's guard when one is dealing with that gang of ruffians. They'll beat one up and take one's money. One needs to be smart and keep one's distance.

Note that the possessive form of *one* requires an apostrophe: *one's*.

Demonstrative Pronouns

Demonstrative pronouns make up a small group. They are *this, that, these, those*, and *such*. *This* and *that* are singular, *these* and *those* are plural, and *such* can be either singular or plural. Like other third-person pronouns, the demonstrative pronouns can replace a noun or noun phrase. But they are also used as *determiners*. That is, they can act as a modifier of a noun. When the noun and any other accompanying modifiers are removed, the determiners then function as pronouns:

Determiner	Pronoun
This old house belongs to my uncle.	**This** belongs to my uncle.
Are you going to wear **that** funny hat?	Are you going to wear **that**?
Who took **those** new DVDs?	Who took **those**?
These nursery rhymes make me laugh.	**These** make me laugh.
Such ideas are my firm beliefs.	**Such** are my firm beliefs.

Demonstrative pronouns functioning as determiners can be used with both animate and inanimate nouns. When used as pronoun replacements, they retain the animate or inanimate meaning of the nouns they replace:

This boy is my nephew.	This is my nephew.
That pen was a gift from Jean.	That was a gift from Jean.
These people should be arrested.	These should be arrested.
Those logs should be removed.	Those should be removed.

Just using *this*, *that*, *these*, or *those* alone does not always make sense. By adding *one(s)* to these pronouns, a more specific meaning is derived and an awkward statement is avoided:

This girl threw the snowball.	This **one** threw the snowball.
I want that big candy bar.	I want that **one**.
These pancakes don't taste right.	These **ones** don't taste right.
Mark chose those black slacks.	Mark chose those **ones**.

Because the word *one* identifies a single entity, its plural form *ones* sounds awkward, and many people avoid its use and use the demonstrative pronoun alone.

Indefinite Pronouns

Indefinite pronouns are not substitutes for specific nouns. Instead they stand for people or things *in general*. Some of the commonly used indefinite pronouns are:

all	everybody	one
anybody	everything	some
each	none	somebody

Note that *anybody, everybody,* and *somebody* can be said as *anyone, everyone,* and *someone.*

All and *some* are singular or plural, depending upon to what or to whom they refer. The others are always singular:

Singular or Plural
All was spent on a big party. (all the money = singular)
All are accounted for. (all the soldiers = plural)

There is some on the table for you. (some bread = singular)
Some were forced to pay higher taxes. (some citizens = plural)

Always Singular
Is anybody at home?
Each has to get up and sing a song.
Everybody knows that she's the most competent in our department.
Everything was finally repaired.
One fell off a swing and was injured.
Somebody wants to go out with Laura.

There are several other words that function both as determiners and indefinite pronouns. These are *any, both, either, enough, few, fewer, less, little, many, more, much, neither,* and *several.* Let's look at a few pairs of sentences that illustrate their use as determiners and as indefinite pronouns:

I'll accept any books you want to get rid of.
I'll accept any you want to get rid of.

Do you have enough money?
Do you have enough?

Fewer citizens voted in the last election.
Fewer voted in the last election.

Neither woman was chosen to be the new CEO.
Neither was chosen to be the new CEO.

Relative Pronouns

Relative pronouns are used to connect two clauses in which the same noun or pronoun appears. A relative pronoun replaces one of the nouns or pronouns in the two clauses. For example:

John is my best friend. John moved to Miami.
John, who moved to Miami, is my best friend.

The English relative pronouns are *who (whom, whose), which,* and *that.* The forms of *who* refer to people, *which* refers to things, and *that* usually refers to things but can also refer to people.

There is a difference in how these relative pronouns function. *That* is used to introduce a *restrictive* relative clause, which is not set off by commas. *Who* and *which* are used to introduce a *non-restrictive* relative clause, which is set off by commas. The pronoun *who* can also be used in restrictive relative clauses.

Restrictive relative clauses provide essential meaning that further describes the antecedent of the relative pronoun. For example:

I actually met a man that stole a million dollars. *or* I actually met a man who stole a million dollars. (The man's reputation as a thief is essential information.)

She threw away the ring that I spent my last dollar on. (The money that I spent on the ring is essential information.)

Non-restrictive clauses provide parenthetical, non-essential information.

The judge, who lived many years in Canada, was granted a quick divorce. (Where the judge lived in the past does not affect the meaning of the base sentence.)

I found an old necklace, which had once belonged to a princess. (To whom the necklace belonged is not essential information.)

Use *whom* if the relative pronoun is used as an object in the relative clause. Use *whose* if it is used as a possessive:

The baritone, to whom we sent a bottle of champagne, gave a magnificent performance.

We visited my cousin, whose son is studying to be a doctor, in Arizona.

With the suffix *-ever*, indefinite relative pronouns are derived: *whoever*, *whomever*, and *whatever*. The antecedent for these pronouns is understood and not included in the sentence:

Whoever gets 75 percent on this test will pass the course. (The person who gets 75 percent on this test will pass the course.)

The boss chose whomever he wanted for the promotion. (The boss chose the person whom he wanted for the promotion.)

He was rich and bought whatever he liked. (He was rich and bought everything that he liked.)

What can also function as an indefinite relative pronoun. It replaces *that* and *which*.

This brochure will explain what you need to do. (This brochure will explain that which you need to know.)

She sent me what I really wanted. (She sent me that which I really wanted.)

Reflexive Pronouns

The reflexive pronouns are counterparts to the personal pronouns. They are:

	Subjective	**Objective**	**Reflexive**
First-person singular	I	me	myself
Second-person singular	you (*sing.*)	you	yourself
Third-person singular	he	him	himself
Third-person singular	she	her	herself
Third-person singular	it	it	itself
First-person plural	we	us	ourselves
Second-person plural	you (*pl.*)	you	yourselves
Third-person plural	they	them	themselves
Third-person singular	one	one	oneself

Reflexive pronouns are used as objects in a sentence when the subject and the object are the same person or thing. If the subject and object are not the same person or thing, the objective form of the personal pronoun is used. For example:

I bought **her** a new sweater.
I bought **myself** a new sweater.

Does he ever doubt **me**?
Does he ever doubt **himself**?

The men protected **us** from the scorching heat.
The men protected **themselves** from the scorching heat.

When a compound subject is formed with the first-person singular *I*, the first-person plural reflexive pronoun should be used:

Several of the girls and I promised **ourselves** a long afternoon at a spa.

See Chapter 8 for reflexive pronouns used with reflexive verbs.

Intensive Pronouns

Intensive pronouns look like reflexive pronouns, but they function differently. They tend to follow a noun or pronoun and give it *emphasis*:

I myself don't believe he committed the crime.
Ms. Brown herself waited in the rain for the train to arrive.

These pronouns can also appear at the end of a sentence, sometimes preceded by the preposition *by*, and suggest that someone is performing an action *on his* or *her own*:

Five-year-old Sarah made her bed herself.
Why did Michael want to go to the library by himself?

Reciprocal Pronouns

The reciprocal pronouns are *one another* and *each other*. They are used to combine two sentences in which the action of the verb is identical in both. The direct objects or indirect objects of the two sentences are replaced by either of the reciprocal pronouns, and the sentences are combined as one. The verbs in sentences with reciprocal pronouns are always *plural*. For example:

My girlfriend loves me. I love my girlfriend.
My girlfriend and I love **each other**. (direct object)
My girlfriend and I love **one another**.

John buys Mary some new gloves. Mary buys John some new gloves.
John and Mary buy **one another** some new gloves. (indirect object)
John and Mary buy **each other** some new gloves.

Reciprocal pronouns can also be used as the object of a preposition or to show possession:

They sent Valentine cards **to** one another (to each other).
The women admired one **another's** gowns (each other's gowns).

Interrogative Pronouns

The interrogative pronouns *who*, *which*, and *what* ask, respectively, about a person, about a choice, and about a thing. The answer can be in noun or pronoun form:

Who ordered the steak?	I did.
Whom did you meet in Toledo?	We met John.
Which should I choose?	Take the one covered in chocolate.
Which do you prefer?	I really prefer the silk scarf.
What on earth is that?	That's a tropical beetle.
What did you buy?	An overcoat.

Interrogative pronouns can also function as determiners. For example:

Whose car did he borrow?	He borrowed Mary's car.
Which words did he misspell?	He misspelled *neighbor* and *trophy*.
What problems gave you trouble?	The problems on geometry.

There is a difference between *which* and *what* that is not always clear. *Which* is used to distinguish people or things:

Which man?	The one in the blue coat.
Which painting?	The one by Rembrandt.

What inquires into the kind or the category of something:

What books do you read?	I read science fiction.
What foods can't she eat?	Anything with dairy in it.

14. Plurals

Many English words form their plural by the addition of a final *-s*. This simple plural ending is used following most consonant sounds, even when the final letter is a silent *-e*. The plural ending *-s* is also found after vowel sounds, even when the spelling of a word with a final vowel sound ends with *-y*, *-e*, or other silent letter:

Consonant	***-y* and *-e***	**Silent Letter**
songs	toys	sighs
cakes	lies	plows

Words that end in a consonant followed by *-y* change the *-y* to *-ie* and then add *-s*:

candy → candies
lady → ladies
pony → ponies

If a noun ends with the sound *-s*, *-z*, *-ch*, *-dg*, or *-sh*, the plural ending will be *-es* and will be pronounced as an individual syllable:

case → cases
size → sizes
catch → catches
edge → edges
flash → flashes

Some English words do not use an *-s* in the formation of a plural. Their plural formations are irregular:

child → children   foot → feet
goose → geese   louse → lice
man → men   mouse → mice
ox → oxen   tooth → teeth
woman → women

Another irregular plural form occurs in nouns that end in *-f* or *-fe*. The letters *-f* or *-fe* change to *-ves* to form the plural:

calf → calves
elf → elves
half → halves
hoof → hooves
knife → knives
leaf → leaves
life → lives
scarf → scarfs/scarves
shelf → shelves
thief → thieves
wife → wives
wolf → wolves

When a noun ends in *-o*, the plural formation is not constant for all words. Some words form the plural with *-s*, while others form the plural with *-es*. For example:

Plural with *-os*	Plural with *-oes*
auto → autos	echo → echoes
kilo → kilos	hero → heroes
memo → memos	potato → potatoes
photo → photos	tomato → tomatoes
piano → pianos	torpedo → torpedoes
solo → solos	veto → vetoes

Some words that end in *-o* can form the plural with either *-os* or *-oes*. For example:

buffalo → buffalos/buffaloes
cargo → cargos/cargoes
mosquito → mosquitos/mosquitoes
motto → mottos/mottoes
tornado → tornados/tornadoes
volcano → volcanos/volcanoes

Certain nouns are irregular in that they use the same form in the both the singular and plural, yet the noun always appears to be a plural noun. For example:

Singular	Plural
one barracks	five barracks
one crossroads	five crossroads
one headquarters	five headquarters
one species	five species

Other nouns use the same form in both the singular and plural, yet the noun always appears to be a singular noun. For example:

Singular	Plural
one deer	ten deer
one fish	ten fish
one offspring	ten offspring
one sheep	ten sheep

Interestingly, the names of many fish follow this pattern. For example: *cod, halibut, perch, trout,* and *tuna.* A notable exception is *shark → sharks.*

Nouns that end in *-is* form their plural by changing *-is* to *-es*:

analysis → analyses
basis → bases
crisis → crises
emphasis → emphases
neurosis → neuroses
oasis → oases
parenthesis → parentheses
synopsis → synopses
thesis → theses

There are many foreign words in English. They tend to retain the plural form of the foreign language. However, some have also developed an English plural form that is used just as much as the foreign plural:

Latin Nouns That End in -*a*	Latin Plural	English Plural
antenna	antennae	antennas
formula	formulae	formulas
larva	larvae	N/A
nebula	nebulae	nebulas
vertebra	vertebrae	N/A

Latin Nouns That End in -*ex*/-*ix*	Latin Plural	English Plural
appendix	appendices	appendixes
cervix	cervices	cervixes
index	indices	indexes
matrix	matrices	matrixes
vortex	vortices	N/A

Latin Nouns That End in *-us*	Latin Plural	English Plural
alumnus	alumni	N/A
cactus	cacti	cactuses
fungus	fungi	funguses
nucleus	nuclei	N/A
octopus	octopi	octopuses

Latin Nouns That End in *-um*	Latin Plural	English Plural
bacterium	bacteria	N/A
curriculum	curricula	curriculums
datum	data	N/A
medium	media	mediums
memorandum	memoranda	memorandums

Words that come from Italian and are commonly used in English retain the Italian plural. For example:

libretto → libretti
paparazzo → paparazzi
tempo → tempi
virtuoso → virtuosi

15. Modifiers

Modifiers are words that help to describe other words. There are *adjectival* modifiers and *adverbial* modifiers. Adjectives modify nouns and pronouns, and adverbs modify verbs, adjectives, and other adverbs.

Adjectives

Adjectives can be *attributive* adjectives or *predicate* adjectives. Attributive adjectives precede the noun they modify:

The **old** man sat near the **drafty** window.
A **wealthy** woman gave the boy a **gold** coin.

Predicate adjectives follow linking verbs and modify noun or pronoun subjects from their position in the predicate:

He seemed **old** although he was not yet forty.
Mrs. Johnson was always **wealthy**.

You have already encountered definite and indefinite articles in Chapter 12 and determiners in Chapter 13. Both articles and determiners are types of attributive adjectives. They modify the meaning of nouns. For example:

a man	the man	this man	that man
some children	the children	these children	those children

Adjectives that are of similar type can be listed in categories. One of these categories is composed of *quantifiers*. These are adjectives that describe a quantity, such as *many, more, much, less,* and *numerous*. For example:

He has **several** questions to ask of the mayor.
Few students could agree with the professor's remarks.
I rarely have **lots** of free time on my hands.

Another category of adjectives describes a *characteristic* of a noun or pronoun. These are often the opinion of the writer or speaker:

Mr. Snyder was such a **horrible** man.
I couldn't bear another minute of that **boring** lecture.
Brad Pitt's new movie is **fantastic**!

Some adjectives are *adjectives of quality*. They describe age, color, size, or other qualities of a person or object:

The **little** girls were playing with an **expensive** doll.
That **white** house is where **old** Mr. Jones lives.
I want to order a **large** pizza, please.

Some adjectives are *derived from nouns*. The general meaning of the noun is retained but is modified by a suffix or prefix. A common suffix is *-ly*:

friend   Tom is such a **friendly** fellow.
time   We got the job done in a **timely** fashion.
day   My **daily** routine begins with a jog through the park.

A prefix commonly used to form an adjective is the letter *a-*. Adjectives derived in this way tend to be predicate adjectives and follow the verb *to be*:

blaze   The park was **ablaze** with fireworks and campfires.
drift   Their boat is **adrift** in the rushing waters of the river.
live   I think the goldfish are still **alive**.

Adjectives of substance describe the material from which something is made:

He stirred the stew with a **wooden** spoon.
We ate our dinner on **plastic** plates.
The queen was bathing in a **golden** tub.

When two or more words are combined to form an adjective, that adjective is called a *compound adjective*. The words that compose a compound adjective can be most any part of speech:

The **three-month-old** pups were taken from their mother.
I was invited to their house for **Christmas Eve** dinner.
Mr. Phillips needs to make a **long-distance** call.

Numbers can be used as adjectives. They are different from quantifiers in that they describe a specific amount (*one, fourteen, six hundred*) rather than a general amount (*few, many, several*). Number-adjectives can be cardinal numbers (*one, two*) or ordinal numbers (*first, second*):

I need **five** orders of French fries and **seven** cans of Coke.
Little Billy is now in the **third** grade.
Those earrings cost a **thousand** dollars!

Adjectives of time describe not only the time on a clock but any interval of time or frequency of time:

We took the **six o'clock** train to Boston.
Our **September** meeting has to be postponed two weeks.
Their **frequent** bickering made them unwelcome guests.

As described in Chapter 7, *present and past participles* can be used as adjectives:

The flamingo's **flapping** wings alerted the other birds to the danger.
Your bicycle is **broken** again and can't be repaired.
Her son, **singing** merrily in the shower, was accepted to Harvard today.

Many adjectives describe an *origin* or *nationality*:

Germany and France belong to the **European** Union.
French wine is sometimes too expensive for us.
I'm really interested in **South American** history.

English uses *nouns as adjectives* in abundance. The nouns make no changes and add no endings; they are used just as they appear in noun form. These noun-adjectives can be either common nouns or proper nouns:

Common Nouns Used as Adjectives
The **trade** unions will meet next week.
I need to get the latest **bus** schedule.
My uncle runs a little **vegetable** stand in the summer.

Proper Nouns Used as Adjectives
The *Chicago Sun Times* is a daily newspaper.
Where can we get a bottle of **India** ink?
Let's go to the **Wisconsin** state fair.

Just as nouns can be used as adjectives, adjectives can be used as nouns. Such adjectives do not change their form or add endings:

The **rich** just seem to get richer.
The song says that America is the home of the **brave**.
This large building is a home for the **elderly**.

When more than one adjective is used to modify a noun or pronoun, a comma is used to separate the adjectives if they are of the same type (adjectives of substance, time, quality, origin, quantity, and so on). You can check whether or not to use a comma by placing *and* between the adjectives. If the sentence still makes sense, a comma is required. For example:

It was a horrible, boring lecture. (*horrible and boring*)
They just bought a big, sleek car. (*big and sleek*)

But adjectives of different types require no comma between them:

Jim wants to buy a small Italian car. (adjectives of quality and origin)
He acquired several Roman coins. (adjectives of quantity and origin)

Adverbs

Adverbs modify verbs, adjectives, and other adverbs. They are formed most often by adding the suffix *-ly* to an adjective:

slow → slowly
clear → clearly
smooth → smoothly

Adjectives that end in *-ic* form adverbs by the suffix *-ically*:

historic → historically
basic → basically
romantic → romantically

If an adjective ends in a consonant followed by *-y*, the suffix becomes *-ily*. If the adjective ends in a vowel followed by *-y*, the ending remains just *-ly*:

happy → happily
coy → coyly
merry → merrily

In a few cases, words that end in *-ly* are used both as adjectives and adverbs:

early   yearly   daily

And the adjective *fast* is also the adverbial form of that word:

He's a fast talker. (adjective)
He talks fast. (adverb)

Like adjectives, adverbs occur as types. The five types of adverbs are adverbs of time, adverbs of frequency, adverbs of manner, adverbs of degree, and adverbs of comment. Adverbs can be individual words or a combination of words.

Adverbs of time tell when something is occurring:

We'll join you in London **next week**.
I hope to arrive home **soon**.
The train pulled into the station **a little past midnight**.

Adverbs of frequency tell how often something occurs:

Bob **usually** gets up before 7 A.M.
I drive to Milwaukee **several times a week**.
Mary **sometimes** takes the subway to work.

Adverbs of manner describe how something is done:

The chauffeur **quickly** pulled the car to the curb.
Little Sally pronounced each word in the sentence **carefully**.
John **lazily** dragged himself from the bed to the bathroom.

Adverbs of degree describe how much, how little, or with what intensity something is done. Some commonly used adverbs of degree are *adequately, almost, entirely, extremely, greatly, highly, immensely, moderately, partially, perfectly, practically, totally, tremendously,* and *very.* Let's look at some example sentences:

Mr. Brown was an **immensely** popular teacher.
The sound of her voice was **perfectly** lovely.
The elderly man spoke **very** slowly.

Adverbs of comment provide an opinion or commentary about something. They occur primarily at the beginning of a sentence and are set off by a comma:

Luckily, I had an umbrella along and stayed dry during the storm.
Unfortunately, the concert had to be cancelled.
With much happiness, I wish to announce the birth of my first
  daughter.

In order to use adverbs effectively, they must be placed appropriately in a sentence. Use these general rules for adverb placement:

1. Adverbs of time are placed after the verb or at the end of the sentence. She invited us **last week**.

2. Adverbs of frequency are placed before the main verb but after an auxiliary. He **seldom** comes home late. She has **often** helped me in the garden.

3. Adverbs of manner are placed after the verb or at the end of the sentence. The lecturer speaks **quickly**.

4. Adverbs of degree are placed after the verb or at the end of the sentence but precede the word they modify. His statement was **totally** false.

5. Adverbs of comment are placed at the beginning of a sentence. **Fortunately**, John got a raise the day he bought his new car.

16. Comparatives and Superlatives

The base form of an adjective or adverb is called the *positive* form. Nearly all adjectives and adverbs can be changed to the *comparative* and *superlative* forms. The comparative provides a comparison between two people or things. The superlative describes the greatest degree of the meaning of the adjective or adverb.

Adjectives

To form the comparative and superlative of many adjectives, add the suffix *-er* to the adjective for the comparative and the suffix *-est* for the superlative. If the adjective ends in a consonant followed by *-y*, change the *-y* to *-i*, and then add the suffix. For example:

Positive	Comparative	Superlative
tall	taller	tallest
funny	funnier	funniest
coy	coyer	coyest

If an adjective is a long word, a word derived from a foreign source (particularly Latin), or formed with the suffix *-ing*, the comparative is formed by preceding the adjective with the word *more*. The superlative is formed by preceding the adjective with *most*:

Positive	Comparative	Superlative
boring	more boring	most boring
factual	more factual	most factual
interesting	more interesting	most interesting

A few adjectives form their comparative and superlative in an irregular way:

Positive	Comparative	Superlative
good	better	best
bad	worse	worst
far	farther/further	farthest/furthest
little	less	least
much/many	more	most

The adjective *far* has two forms in the comparative and superlative. Some believe that the two forms can be used interchangeably. But the general rule is that *farther* is the comparative of *far* when it describes physical distance (yards, miles, kilometers), and *further* is the comparative when *far* means an advancement in degree, such as of time or of an amount:

Physical Distance
The village is far from here.
Their house is farther from the station than ours.
Which Illinois college is the farthest from Chicago?

Advancement in Degree
I didn't read very far in that book.
You have to read further to understand the characters.
Jack has read the furthest in the book of anyone in our class.

When using a comparative in a sentence, *than* is used to separate the two words that are being compared. For example:

Robert is shorter **than** Mike.
Does Tina like ice cream better **than** cake?
This novel is more interesting **than** that novel.

The word *than* is considered to be both a conjunction and a preposition. Depending upon which function is involved, the word or phrase that follows *than* can appear in the objective case or the subjective case:

My sister sings better than **me**. (prepositional use)
My sister sings better than **I** (do). (conjunctional use)

When using an adjective in the superlative, the article *the* is placed before the superlative adjective:

This apple pie is **the** best I've ever eaten!
Tom is **the** most talented member of the soccer team.
This sweater is **the** cheapest.

Note: Adjectives that are preceded by *most* in the superlative can show an opposite meaning by preceding them with *least*:

She is the **most** talented. She is the **least** talented.
This dessert is the **most** delicious. This dessert is the **least** delicious.

It has already been stated that nearly all adjectives can be changed to the comparative and superlative. However, the meaning of certain adjectives does not lend itself to these formations. They may occur in the comparative or superlative, but only because they are used figuratively or whimsically. For example:

dead   This battery is **deader** than I thought. This party is the **deadest**.

These comparative and superlative forms would not normally be used to describe a person's death.

Adverbs

When adverbs end in *-ly*, the comparative and superlative are formed by preceding them with *more* and *most*, respectively:

Positive	Comparative	Superlative
quickly	more quickly	most quickly
carefully	more carefully	most carefully
loudly	more loudly	most loudly

In sentences, the comparative and superlative look like this:

Phillip ran **more slowly** than Thomas. Thomas ran **the most slowly**.
She spoke **more angrily** than before. She spoke **the most angrily**.
Laura now sang **more confidently**. Laura sang **the most confidently**.

A note of caution: It is possible to omit *the* from the superlative adverb. However the meaning is changed, and the adverb is no longer in the superlative. The word *most* then means *very*.

Laura sang **most confidently**. (Laura sang very confidently.)

If an adverb does not have the adverbial suffix *-ly*, the comparative and superlative are formed respectively with the suffixes *-er* and *-est*.

Positive	Comparative	Superlative
early	earlier	earliest
fast	faster	fastest
hard	harder	hardest

Remember that *early* is both an adjective and adverb, and the ending *-ly* on the word is not a suffix.

The irregularities of adjectives in the comparative and superlative are the same for adverbs. Let's look at some example sentences:

He walked **better** with a brace on his leg. He walked **the best** in slippers.

Jane ran **worse** than in the first race. Sue ran **the worst** again.

Tim practiced **more** than me. Jack practiced **the most**.

17. Prepositions

Prepositions introduce prepositional phrases. The object of the preposition in such phrases can be a noun or a pronoun. A prepositional phrase describes *where*, *when*, *why*, or *how* of the subject or object of a sentence:

It's a letter **from** Mr. Brown.
John is **with** her.

The following list contains the most commonly used prepositions and their use with a noun or pronoun:

Preposition	Usage	Example
about	description of a topic	It was a story about a little girl.
above	located overhead	The attic is above the second floor.
across	on or to the other side	The hotel is across the river.
among	in the midst of	She sat among the other guests.
at	during a specific time	at one o'clock, at night, at dinner
	next to or by	at the window, at the corner
	age	I became a citizen at thirty.
	in a place	at the store, at the movies
before	earlier than	I arrived before noon.
	in front of	The teacher stood before her new class.
below	lower than, underneath	The pots and pans are kept below the sink.
beside	next to	Mary remained beside her husband.
besides	in addition to	Besides John, no one voted for the plan.
between	space separating two objects	There's an urn between the piano and the door.
by	at the latest	I'll be home by 7 P.M.
	next to	Your bike is by the back door.
	creator of something	This is a painting by Picasso.

Preposition	Usage	Example
for	over a period of time	We lived in Boston for six years.
	on account of	Tim was punished for lying.
	presented to	This is a gift for Helen.
from	given by	We received a card from Uncle Fred.
	due to	Bill got ill from spoiled meat.
	at the starting point	We drove from Toledo to Cleveland.
in	during periods of time	in June, in summer, in 2010, in the morning
	located inside	Jean stayed in her room.
	entering a vehicle	I got in the car. Bob got in a taxi.
	within a period of time	The package arrived here in four days.
	after a period of time	I can be back in two weeks.
into	going to the inside	The children came into the kitchen.
	becoming	The witch turned him into a frog.
next to	beside, adjacent to	The hotel is next to the bus station.
of	about	They spoke of the coming election.
	pertaining to	This is a book of folk tales.
	belonging to	That man is the father of the bride.
off (of)	leaving transport	They get off the train in New York.
	descend	We have to get off of the mountain by dark.
on	boarding transport	I got on the bus. She got on the train.
	attached to	I put a picture of her on the wall.
onto	moving to the top	The woman crawled onto the roof.
out (of)	exiting	She came out the door. I got out of the cab.
over	covered by	John held an umbrella over their heads.

Preposition	Usage	Example
	more than	Is your sister over forty years old?
	getting to the other side	I was walking over the bridge when I fell.
past	minutes after the hour	It's a quarter past nine.
	after a certain time	It's already past your bedtime.
since	from a certain time	since May, since 1999, since the day you arrived
through	in one end, out the other	We ran scared through the dark tunnel.
	until	I'll be in France through the end of June.
till/until	to a certain time, up to	They waited till dawn before they escaped.
to	minutes before the hour	It's ten to seven.
	moving toward	to the car, to school, to the store, to Jim's house
toward(s)	leading to	We moved slowly toward the dark room.
	facing	I looked towards the hill and saw her coming.
under	lower than, beneath	The cat likes to sleep under the bed.
underneath	under, beneath	There's a treasure hidden underneath this floor.

Some prepositions are called *compound prepositions* because they are composed of more than one word. You have already encountered a few of these words in the previous section (*next to, off of,* and *out of*). The words in compound prepositions can be gerunds, nouns, or prepositions. It is the entire compound phrase that has a specific meaning and not the individual words in the compound. For example, *next to* is composed of the words *next* (meaning *subsequent*) and *to* (meaning *moving toward*). But the combination of these words has the meaning *beside* or *adjacent to*.

Preposition	Usage	Example
according to	as stated by	According to Tom, there's no school today.
alongside of	next to, at the side of	They picnicked alongside of the river.
because of	caused by, due to	Her speech was cancelled because of her illness.

Preposition	Usage	Example
by means of	the method for	He solved the problem by means of new calculations.
by way of	using a certain path	We usually come here by way of the interstate.
contrary to	in contradiction of	Contrary to your wishes, we're staying right here.
for the sake of	in the interest of	I omitted this phrase for the sake of clarity.
in accordance with	in agreement with	In accordance with your father's wishes, his portrait will be placed over the mantle.
in addition to	besides	In addition to Joan, Mary will join the team.
in case of	if there is	In case of fire, immediately pull the fire alarm.
in danger of	there is a risk	This project is in danger of failing
in favor of	for	Everyone voted in favor of Jack's suggestion.
in front of	before	There's a strange man in front of our house.
in need of	being necessary	We are very much in need of some rest.
in place of	replacing	They chose John in place of Bob as captain.
in spite of	despite, even though	In spite of my warning, they left on the hike.
in view of	considering	In view of your illness, you cannot go back to work so soon.
instead of	as an alternative	Instead of arguing, you should find something to agree upon.
on account of	caused by, due to	I can't meet with you on account of another appointment.

18. Relative Pronouns

The English relative pronouns are *who* (*whom, whose*), *which*, and *that*. When using the relative pronouns to combine sentences, it is important to know whether the relative clause is restrictive or non-restrictive.

Restrictive Relative Clauses

A relative clause is called restrictive when it provides essential information about the antecedent. When referring to persons, the relative pronoun *that* is used. However, *who* can often function in restrictive relative clauses. Let's look at some examples:

The man **that robbed me** is standing right over there.

The phrase *that robbed me* is essential to the meaning of the sentence and describes the man.

The surgeon **who carried out the operation** is only thirty years old.

Again, the phrase *who carried out the operation* is essential to the sentence and describes the antecedent *the surgeon*.

When referring to inanimate antecedents, *that* is again used in restrictive relative clauses. For example:

The car **that you sold me** doesn't run!

The phrase *that you sold me* describes the car and is essential information.

If a preposition is used with the relative pronoun *that*, the preposition will follow the verb and its object (if any).

The house that I was born **in** burned down last night.
The woman that Bill worked **for** for ten years fired him yesterday.

When *that* is used as a direct object, indirect object, or the object of a preposition, it can be omitted from the relative clause and is understood:

The car you sold me doesn't run!
The house I was born in burned down last night.

Non-Restrictive Relative Clauses

Non-restrictive relative clauses use *who* (*whom, whose*) and *which* as their relative pronouns. They are always set off by commas. These clauses do not provide essential information. The information in the relative clauses is incidental or parenthetical and does not affect the meaning of the sentence. A form of *who* is used to refer to animate antecedents, and *which* is used to refer to inanimate antecedents:

> The mayor, **who was educated in England,** lost last night's election.
> (Where the mayor was educated has nothing to do with the election.)
> The books, **which were donated to the library years ago**, have been lost. (When the books were donated has nothing to do with their having been lost.)

When non-restrictive relative pronouns are introduced by a preposition, the preposition usually precedes the pronoun, but it can also follow the verb and its object (if any):

> Their manager, **for** whom I was planning a party, will travel to Brazil.
> Their manager, whom I was planning a party **for**, will travel to Brazil.

> Your dress, **about** which I was telling my friends, has a large stain on it.
> Your dress, which I was telling my friends **about**, has a large stain on it.

It is very common to use *who* in place of *whom* in the objective case.

Whoever and *What* as Relative Pronouns

When the antecedent of a relative pronoun is persons or things in general, a form of *whoever* or *what* is used. *Whoever* is a stand-in for the phrase *the person who*, and *what* is a stand-in for the phrase *the thing which*. These relative pronouns can occur as subjects or objects:

> **Subject:** Whoever scratched my car will have to pay for the repair.
> **Direct object:** You can dance with whomever you like.

> **Subject:** What you're saying makes no sense at all.
> **Object:** He agreed to what Tina had suggested earlier.

19. Negatives

The most common negative in English is the adverb *not*. It is used to negate verbs or complete predicates.

Negating Verbs

The verbs *to be* and *to have* are negated by placing *not* after them. *To have* can be negated in this way whether used as a transitive verb or as an auxiliary:

I am **not** interested in that.

He has **not** any money left.

They were **not** the winners of
the game.

Bill has **not** seen Jane since May.

It is more common to negate *to have*, when it is used as a transitive verb, with a form of *do not*:

He **does not** have any money
left.

I **did not** have a good time at the
party.

This use of a form of *do not* occurs with all other negated verbs (excluding modal auxiliaries) in the present and past tenses:

We **do not** belong to a country club.
My sister **does not** work in Chicago anymore.
The men **did not** go out on strike.

If the object in a sentence is a plural or a collective noun, *any* precedes the object when the sentence is negated. The modifier *some* often accompanies the object. Let's look at some examples:

We saw children playing in the park. (plural)
We **did not see any** children playing in the park.

Tim has some flowers for her. (plural)
Tim **does not have any** flowers for her.

I need to borrow some money. (collective)
I **do not need to borrow any** money.

Negating Specific Elements of a Sentence

The phrase *not . . . but* can be used to identify a specific negated element in a sentence and the replacement of that negated element:

Negated Direct Object
He did **not buy a car**

Replacement of Direct Object
but a truck.

Let's look at some other example sentences that illustrate the negation of other elements of a sentence:

Negated Prepositional Phrase
Your briefcase is **not in the bedroom**

Replacement of Prepositional Phrase
but in the dining room.

Negated Subject
Not John

Replacement of Subject
but Larry was elected chairman of the committee.

Negated Indirect Object
I **did not give Jim** the money

Replacement of Indirect Object
but Jane.

Neither . . . Nor

When two subjects are negated and are carrying out the same action, *neither* and *nor* are used to introduce those subjects. If the subjects are singular, a singular verb will follow the two subjects. If one or both of the subjects are plural, a plural verb will follow the two subjects:

Neither Tina nor Mary has arrived yet. (singular subjects = singular verb)
Neither the men nor the women like this movie. (plural subjects = plural verb)

This *neither/nor* combination can be used with objects of a sentence, but it is more common to form a negative with *not* and use *either/or* in place of *neither/nor*:

I found neither a book nor a magazine I liked. (possible)
I didn't find either a book or a magazine I liked. (more common)

Other Negatives

There are several other negative expressions that occur in pairs. One negative in the pair is formed from *no*. The other negative in the pair is formed with *not any*:

No	*Not Any*
no one	not anyone
nobody	not anybody
none	not any
nothing	not anything
nowhere	not anywhere

Let's look at some example sentences:

I knew no one at the party.	I did not know anyone at the party.
Jim spoke with nobody.	Jim did not speak with anybody.
She has nothing to say.	She does not have anything to say.
The book is nowhere to be found.	The book is not anywhere to be found.

Although not formed precisely in the same way, the pair *never / not ever* functions in the same manner as the pairs listed previously:

I never play chess with her.	I do not ever play chess with her.

Many negatives can be part of a contraction. For details on contractions, see Chapter 22.

20. Interrogative Pronouns and Exclamations

The interrogative pronouns are used to introduce a question. They appear at the beginning of a sentence. Some refer exclusively to people: *who*, *whom*, and *whose*. *What* refers to objects, and *which* can refer to either people or objects.

Who, Whom, and Whose

If the interrogative pronoun is used as the subject of the sentence and concerns a person, use *who*:

Who solved this difficult problem?
Who won yesterday's election?

If the interrogative is the direct object, indirect object, or the object of a preposition, use *whom*. When *whom* stands for an indirect object, it is preceded by the prepositions *to* or *for* and is the object of one of those prepositions.

Whom did you invite to the dance? (direct object)
To whom are they going to give first prize? (indirect object)
From whom did you get those beautiful roses? (object of a preposition)

It is very common in casual speech to replace *whom* with *who* and to place any preposition at the end of the clause:

Who did you invite to the dance?
Who are they going to give first prize to?
Who did you get those beautiful roses from?

Use *whose* to inquire into ownership. But remember that this is an interrogative pronoun and replaces a noun. A noun should not follow *whose*.

Three horses ran in the race. Whose won the race?
His son and my son both got scholarships. Whose is the smarter son?

What

The interrogative pronoun *what* has only one form and can be the subject or object in a sentence:

> What is that? (subject)
> What caused that horrible accident? (subject)
> What did you buy at the flea market? (direct object)
> In what will you hide the money? (object of a preposition)

In casual speech, the preposition from a prepositional phrase is placed at the end of the clause:

> What will you hide the money in?

Which

The interrogative pronoun *which* has one form and asks for a distinction between two or more persons or things. *Which* can act as the subject or an object in a sentence:

> You have two dogs. Which is your favorite? (subject)
> Mary bought four dresses. Which will she wear to the prom?
>   (direct object)
> Both uncles sent you a gift. From which did you get the perfume?
>   (object of a preposition)

This interrogative pronoun is often accompanied by *one*:

> Which one is your favorite?
> Which one will she wear to the prom?
> From which one did you get the perfume?

In casual speech, the preposition from a prepositional phrase is placed at the end of the clause:

> Which (one) did you get the perfume from?

Exclamations

Exclamations can be complete sentences or individual words. They make an emphatic statement or suggest great surprise. Exclamations are customarily punctuated with an exclamation point:

> That's terrible!
> Go away!

Complete Sentences

Often, the same sentence can be an ordinary statement or an exclamation. Use an exclamation point to identify the sentence as an exclamation, indicating emphasis or surprise:

Look at that ugly dog. (ordinary)
Look at that ugly dog! (emphasis or surprise)

That's amazing. (ordinary)
That's amazing! (emphasis or surprise)

Certain words often introduce an exclamation: *so, such (a), how,* and *what (a).* Use *so* to modify an adjective, use *such a* to modify an adjective followed by a singular noun or with a singular noun alone, and use *such* to modify an adjective followed by a plural or collective noun or with a plural or collective noun alone. For example:

Your daughter is so intelligent!
That idea is so stupid!
Jim is such a liar!
This class is such a terrible bore!
You're talking such nonsense!
I hate such long commercials!

Use *how* to introduce an exclamation that consists of an adverb or adjective followed by a subject and a verb:

How gorgeous you look tonight!
How pitifully mother sobbed!

In many cases, an exclamation is still possible even when omitting modifiers:

How he has grown!
How the fields have withered in the heat!

Use *what a* followed by an adjective and a singular noun or by a singular noun alone:

What a charming girl she has become!
What a shock that was!

Use *what* followed by an adjective and a plural or collective noun or by a plural or collective noun alone:

What great strides you've made!
What idiots!

Interjections

Interjections are individual words or short phrases that can stand alone or introduce a sentence. The interjections are exclamations, even when the sentence they introduce is not:

Ah, this is my lucky day!
Hey! Get away from my car!
My goodness, you look awful!
Oh dear! I think I've stepped on your toes.
Oh, no!
Ouch! That's painful!
Well, you seem to have aged well!
Wow!

21. Conjunctions

Conjunctions are words that connect individual words, groups of words, or entire clauses. For example:

Laura **and** I went to a concert. (individual words combined by *and*)
You will have to take the train **or** rent a car. (groups of words combined by *or*)
It's getting rather late, **but** the children can stay up a bit longer. (clauses combined by *but*)

Coordinating Conjunctions

There are seven coordinating conjunctions: *and, but, for, nor, or, so,* and *yet.* When combining clauses have a subject and predicate in each, a comma is used to separate the clauses. If the elements combined are individual words or groups of words, a comma is not used.

Not all of the coordinating conjunctions can combine words or groups of words as well as clauses. Those that can are *and, but, or,* and *yet*:

The team was playing well, and a large crowd was gathering at the soccer field.
Tom made a chili that was spicy and too tangy for Aunt Mary.

Our retriever loves swimming in the lake, but he hates getting a bath.
The cat likes to sleep under the table but always keeps her tail tucked under.

Should we buy a new television set, or should we go on a vacation?
This stew can be eaten with a fork or with a spoon.

Dad was nervous, yet he let me take the car out alone for the first time.
Jane complains about Bill yet still cares deeply for him.

The remaining coordinating conjunctions—*for, nor,* and *so*—only combine clauses:

I'm very careful with my laptop, for it's much too expensive to replace.

Mr. Kane doesn't like rock and roll, nor does he care much for
    rap music.
Jim knows nothing about cars, so I had to replace the battery for him.

Notice that with the conjunction *nor*, the subject and verb are transposed:

She won't clean the kitchen, nor **will she** help make the beds.
I didn't set my alarm, nor **did I** even think about getting up early
    that day.

Subordinating Conjunctions

When a subordinating conjunction introduces an *independent clause*, that
clause becomes *dependent* and must be attached to a main clause—another
independent clause:

Independent clause: Mary lived in France.
Subordinating conjunction introduces the clause: When Mary lived
    in France.
Dependent clause is added to independent clause: When Mary lived
    in France, she became quite knowledgeable about wine.

There are many subordinating conjunctions. They are derived from other
parts of speech or are even a combination of words. Some of the most commonly used are:

after	even if	that
although	how	though
as	if	till/until
as if	inasmuch	unless
as long as	in order that	until
as much as	lest	when
as soon as	now that	whenever
as though	provided that	where
because	since	wherever
before	so that	while

If a subordinating or dependent clause begins a sentence, a comma will
separate that clause from the independent clause. For example:

Although I don't know you well, I feel I can trust you in this matter.
Now that you're settled in your new home, I hope you'll stop by for
    a visit.
Wherever the boy tried to hide, his dog would always find him.

If the dependent clause follows the independent clause, a comma is not required:

The cadets sat down for a rest after the sergeant blew his whistle.
Jane hid behind a tree as soon as she saw Michael coming down
    the path.
I learned a little German while I was living in Munich.

If the dependent clause is in the middle of the sentence, it must be separated from the sentence by commas:

Every Saturday, after she practices the piano, Jane goes to the movies.
During the summer, while the family is at the lake cottage, John has the
    whole house to himself.

Correlative Conjunctions

Correlative conjunctions are pairs of words that function together as a conjunction. The correlative conjunctions are:

as . . . as	neither . . . nor
both . . . and	either . . . or
not only . . . but also	whether . . . or

These conjunctions combine *equal and parallel* elements of a sentence: a verb with a verb, a noun with a noun, a phrase with a phrase and so on. Let's look at some examples:

That woman is as **tough** with the men as she is **gentle** with the children.
I want both **a new car** and **a new boat**.
You are not only **lying to me** but also **laughing at me**.
Neither **his good deeds** nor **his acts of kindness** were remembered
    after his death.
Either **you help with the dishes** or **you get no allowance this week**.
She doesn't know whether **to kiss him** or **to slap his face**.

Conjunctive Adverbs

When adverbs combine two independent clauses, they are then conjunctive adverbs—conjunctions. Some commonly used conjunctive adverbs are:

accordingly	furthermore	nevertheless
again	hence	otherwise
also	however	still

besides	indeed	that is
consequently	in fact	then
finally	instead	therefore
for example	likewise	thus
further	moreover	

Conjunctive adverbs can act as pure adverbs. When they do, they are not conjunctions:

I planned **accordingly** and had taxi money for the trip home.
Jean cancelled her dental appointment and went to the movies **instead**.

When conjunctive adverbs combine two independent clauses, the first clause ends with a semicolon (;). The clause that follows begins with the conjunctive adverb, followed by a comma. Let's look at some example sentences:

Tom had a headache again; accordingly, he took a couple of aspirin.
My brother isn't much of a swimmer; in fact, he really hates the water.
We didn't visit Uncle Mike on the farm; instead, we took a drive into town.
There is no evidence in this case; therefore, this lawsuit will be dropped.

When clauses are combined by conjunctive adverbs, the intent is to show *a link or relationship* between the ideas in the two clauses. If the clauses are written as separate sentences, the link or relationship between the ideas is more distant and the conjunctive adverb functions as a pure adverb. If the adverb begins the clause, it is separated from the clause by a comma. For example:

The car is old and needs repairs; **nevertheless**, I will buy it for the parts. (conjunctive adverb)
The car is old and needs repairs. **Nevertheless**, I will buy it for the parts. (adverb)
That fellow got a large inheritance; **hence**, he spends money like a play-boy. (conjunctive adverb)
That fellow got a large inheritance. **Hence**, he spends money like a playboy. (adverb)

22. Contractions

A contraction is a word composed of two words, one of which uses an apostrophe in place of an omitted letter or letters. For example, *do not* becomes *don't*.

Many nouns and pronouns can be combined with a present-tense form of the verb *to be*:

Words with No Contraction	Contraction
I am	I'm
you are	you're
he is	he's
she is	she's
it is	it's
someone is	someone's
we are	we're
they are	they're
here is	here's
how is	how's
there is	there's
who is	who's
what is	what's
where is	where's
when is	when's
Bill is	Bill's

Let's look at some example sentences:

She's at work until six o'clock.
There's something wrong with the car.
What's in the basement?

Many words form a contraction with a present-tense or past-tense form of the verb *to have*. This contraction is often used when *to have* is the auxiliary of one of the perfect tenses (*it has been = it's been*).

Words with No Contraction	**Contraction**
I have/had	I've/I'd
you have/had	you've/you'd
he has/had	he's/he'd
she has/had	she's/she'd
it has/had	it's/—
we have/had	we've/we'd
they have/had	they've/they'd
nobody has/had	nobody's/—
how has/have/had	how's/how've/how'd
there has/have/had	there's/there've/there'd
who has/have/had	who's/who've/who'd
what has/have/had	what's/what've/—
when has/have/had	when's/when've/—
where has/have/had	where's/where've/where'd
Mary has/had	Mary's/—

Let's look at some example sentences:

I've got a little secret to tell you.
Where've you been the entire day?
How'd they been able to do that?

Will and *shall* form the same contractions, and contractions of *would* resemble contractions of *had*:

I shall/would	I'll/I'd
you will/would	you'll/you'd
he will/would	he'll/he'd
she will/would	she'll/she'd
it will/would	it'll/—
we shall/would	we'll/we'd
they will/would	they'll/they'd
how will/would	how'll/how'd
who will/would	who'll/who'd
what will/would	what'll/—
where will/would	where'll/where'd
when will/would	when'll/—

Let's look at some example sentences:

He'll be home in time for a late supper.
She's not experienced. Who'd vote for her?
We'd better save more money.

Several contractions are formed with modals followed by the verb *to have*. For example:

I could have	I could've
you should have	you should've
he must have	he must've
we might have	we might've
Tom would have	Tom would've

Many verbs combine with the contracted form of *not*:

are not	aren't
cannot	can't
could not	couldn't
did not	didn't
do not	don't
does not	doesn't
had not	hadn't
has not	hasn't
have not	haven't
is not	isn't
must not	mustn't
need not	needn't
ought not	oughtn't
shall not	shan't
should not	shouldn't
was not	wasn't
were not	weren't
will not	won't
would not	wouldn't

Let's look at some examples:

That doesn't make any sense.
You shouldn't use language like that.
I wouldn't buy such an expensive car.

Note: Some often use *ain't* in place of *isn't* and *aren't*, but *ain't* is an unacceptable form in written English.

Some contractions are from another time and are considered poetical or quaint, but they are still used to make a specific point or to provide the flavor of the past. For example:

'twixt twelve and twenty (between [betwixt] twelve and twenty)
'Tis a miracle. (It's a miracle.)
'Twas the night before Christmas. (It was the night before Christmas.)

If e'er my son / Follow the war . . . (If ever my son were to go to war . . .)
It's five o'clock. (It's five of the clock.)
jack-o'-lantern (jack-of-lantern)
He's a ne'er-do-well. (He is a failure [never does well].)
ma'am (madam)

The expression *let's* is the contraction of *let us*:

Let's take a drive out into the country.
Let's stop at a diner for some lunch.
Let's try to fix that old radio.

23. Possessives

Showing possession with nouns and pronouns is relatively simple in English. However, there are two ways to form possessives with nouns and yet another way to form possessives with pronouns.

Possessive Nouns

One way that nouns become possessive is by adding an *s* with an apostrophe either following or preceding the *s*. Another possessive form is a prepositional phrase introduced by the preposition *of*:

Apostrophe and *s*	**Prepositional Phrase with** *of*
Tom's car	the call of the wild
the boys' teachers	the roar of the motors
Ms. Snyder's office	a bed of roses

There is a tendency to use an apostrophe and *s* with people and a prepositional phrase with *of* with objects. But that is a general rule; there are instances when either form is appropriate. Let's look at some examples that illustrate the general rule:

People	**Objects**
my sister's dress	the color of my car
Robert's new suit	the cost of the wine
his parents' vacation plans	the crackle of the burning logs

Care must be taken with the preposition *of*. It not only shows possession but can be synonymous with the preposition *from* or the phrases *made from* or *consisting of*. For example:

the flag of England (possessive)
citizens of New York (*from*)
a bar of gold (*made from*)
a book of matches (*consisting of*)

With animals or other living creatures, it is often possible to use either possessive form:

the lion's roar	the roar of the lion
the ducks' nest	the nest of the ducks
a camel's humps	the humps of a camel

And a few expressions with inanimate objects can also be formed by either possessive formation. However, if the apostrophe and *s* sound awkward, that formation should be avoided:

the river's edge	the edge of the river
the trumpets' blare	the blare of the trumpets
nighttime's silence	the silence of nighttime

A prepositional phrase introduced by *of* is frequently used with people as the object of the preposition. If a prepositional phrase sounds awkward, that formation should be avoided:

the bride's father	the father of the bride
the girl's parents	the parents of the girl
the workers' wages	the wages of the workers

An apostrophe followed by *s* is used to show a singular possessive. However, if the noun already ends in *s*, an apostrophe is added to the end of the word and a second *s* is optional: *Charles' book* or *Charles's book*. Whichever option is used should be used consistently. Do not use both in the same text.

Singular Noun	**Singular Noun Ending in *s***
father's work schedule	Mr. Jones' car / Mr. Jones's car
Jack's new shoes	James' new hat / James's new hat
Einstein's theory	Carlos' mother / Carlos's mother

If a singular noun ends in a silent *s*, it is customary to add both an apostrophe and additional *s*: *Arkansas's population* and *the Marine Corps's rules*.

Plural nouns that end in *s* are followed by an apostrophe. If the plural formation is irregular, use an apostrophe followed by *s*:

Plural Noun	**Irregular Plural Noun**
my sisters' bedroom	the children's nursery
the bosses' orders	the mice's hiding place
the candidates' speeches	the women's laughter

Although expressions of time are not people, their possessives tend to be formed with an *s* and an apostrophe:

a single day's wages	three years' imprisonment
a good night's sleep	two weeks' vacation
one month's salary	four semesters' tuition

Gerunds

In Chapter 7 gerunds and their use were discussed. They are formed like present participles but function as nouns. It is a common mistake to follow a noun with a present participle when, instead, the noun should be in the possessive and be followed by a gerund. For example:

I can't bear Tom's singing.
We worry about Jean's working so late.
She doesn't like the boys' arguing.

Noun Versus Possessive Noun

Many nouns can be used as adjectives that modify other nouns. However, the same nouns can be formed in the possessive and be used as possessive modifiers. Of course, there is a difference in meaning. If the noun is used without an article, it is an adjective that merely identifies the group or organization for which it stands. If it is a possessive noun, it shows ownership of the noun it modifies. The latter of these can often have another accompanying adjective. Let's look at some example phrases:

Plural Noun	Possessive Noun
former Bears coach Mike Ditka	the Bears' new coach
Walmart greeter Jane Smith	Walmart's greeters are polite.
White House reporter Bill Jones	the White House's new spokesperson

Possessive Adjectives

Possessive adjectives are counterparts of the personal pronouns. They are:

Pronoun	Possessive Adjective
I	my
you	your
he	his
she	her
it	its
we	our
they	their
who	whose

The possessive adjectives modify nouns and precede them like attributive adjectives. For example:

My brother lives with **his** girlfriend's cousin.
Your dog bit **their** little boy.

Our camp site is set up on a small piece of **your** land.
Whose motorcycle is this?

Possessive Pronouns

The possessive pronouns are similar to the possessive adjectives, but they are not modifiers. Possessive pronouns function as pronouns. They are:

Pronoun	Possessive Pronoun
I	mine
you	yours
he	his
she	hers
it	its
we	ours
they	theirs
who	whose

Pronouns replace nouns in a sentence, and possessive pronouns do just that. Compare the following pairs of sentences and take note how a possessive adjective is changed to a possessive pronoun:

Possessive Adjective	Possessive Pronoun
My books were stolen.	**Mine** were stolen.
Is your bike still being repaired?	Is **yours** still being repaired?
Her new baby is really cute.	**Hers** is really cute.
Their wedding will be in June.	**Theirs** will be in June.

Both possessive adjectives and possessive pronouns can be used in special phrases that describe ownership. Although it may seem redundant, both an apostrophe and *s* and the preposition *of* can be used in the same expressions. If the object of the preposition *of* is something other than a person, a possessive adjective can be included in the phrase, but an apostrophe and *s* cannot. For example:

Mr. Garcia is a member **of** the museum staff.
Jane wants to become the captain **of our** team.
Lieutenant Burns is the leader **of their** platoon.

Because the last two examples contain a possessive adjective, the sentences can be rewritten with possessive pronouns replacing the nouns:

Jane wants to become the captain of **ours**.
Lieutenant Burns is the leader of **theirs**.

When a noun is a person and is the object of the preposition *of*, that noun will be formed as a possessive with an apostrophe and *s*:

Jim is a good friend **of my** brother**'s**.
These are the plans **of** the new architect**'s**.
I read and liked those stories **of your** sister**'s**.

Because the final nouns in the previous sentences are in the possessive, the sentences cannot be rewritten with the possessive pronouns provided there. Instead, third-person singular pronouns are used to replace the third-person singular nouns in those sentences:

Jim is a good friend of **his**. (*brother's*)
These are the plans of **his**. (*architect's*)
I read and liked those stories of **hers**. (*sister's*)

The preposition *of* followed by a possessive pronoun can replace a possessive adjective in a sentence. For example:

Possessive Adjective	**Possessive Pronoun**
Marie met **my** good friend.	Marie met a good friend **of mine**.
John and Mike are **their** cousins.	John and Mike are cousins **of theirs**.
They were all **her** students.	They were all students **of hers**.

Compound Possessives

Compound possessives are a combination of two or more nouns. In that combination, one or more of those nouns can be formed in the possessive. Naturally, there is a difference in meaning. For example:

Jane and William's children are playing in the park.

In this sentence, the use of one possessive on the name *William* indicates that the compound *Jane and William* is one possessive. They are the parents of the same children playing in the park.

Jane's and **William's** children are playing in the park.

The sentence shown here has two possessives. This says that Jane has children and William has children, but they are not the same children. Jane and William are not the parents of all the children, only of their own. Let's look at a couple more examples:

Bill and **Frank's** motorboat needs some repairs. (Bill and Frank own the same boat.)
The **Browns'** and the **Smiths'** houses are located in Beverly Hills. (The Browns have a house in Beverly Hills. The Smiths also have a house in Beverly Hills. But they do not own the same house.)

24. Punctuation

The following punctuation marks are used in modern English:

period	.	brackets	[ ]
question mark	?	apostrophe	'
exclamation point	!	hyphen	-
comma	,	dash	—
colon	:	double quotation marks	" "
semicolon	;	single quotation marks	' '
parentheses	( )		

The Period

The period is used to end a declarative or imperative sentence:

Declarative: I expect to be home around suppertime.
Imperative: Please be home around suppertime.

Also use a period to end a sentence that is declarative in nature but that contains the elements of a question:

I wonder whether you have some time to help me today. (**Question:** Do you have some time to help me today?)

A period is used in abbreviations:

Dr. Jones	Ms. Smith	Mr. Brown
etc.	Inc.	Ltd.
A.M.	P.M.	U.S.A.

If a sentence ends with an abbreviation, an additional period is *not* needed to end the sentence:

The train will arrive at 8 P.M.

The Question Mark

The question mark is used to end a question:

Are you sure?
When will they finally arrive?
In what year was your grandfather born?

The Exclamation Point

The exclamation point punctuates a sentence that shows strong emotion or excitement. It is used after a word or phrase that is an exclamation:

Hurry! Get to the basement! A tornado is coming!
A car turned the corner and crashed into the lamppost!
Shut up!
No!

Even if the statement is a question, an exclamation point can be used to show strong emotion or disbelief:

How can that be!
What in the world happened!

The Comma

The comma has a variety of uses, but it can be generalized as separating a series of ideas or separating ideas to avoid confusion. For example:

An American Indian and Englishman entered the race. (In this sentence there are two contestants in the race: American Indian and Englishman.)
An American, Indian, and Englishman entered the race. (In this sentence there are three contestants in the race: American, Indian, and Englishman.)

Use commas to separate adjectives that modify a noun. But do not use commas to separate adverbs.

She wore a pretty, blue dress. (two adjectives: *pretty* and *blue*)
He spoke very carefully about it. (two adverbs: *very* and *carefully*)

If you combine a series of words or phrases with *and, or,* or *neither . . . nor,* commas are not needed:

I bought bread and jam and peanut butter.
That car might be a 2006 or a 2007 or a 2008. I'm not sure.
Neither Bill nor John nor Mary knew about the problem.

Use a comma to separate a subordinate clause from the main clause only if the subordinate clause begins the sentence:

If you have time, you could drop by to visit Aunt Jane.
When the storm began, we all ran to the picnic shelter.

He had no idea how the argument started.
It's unimportant whether you believe me or not.

The conjunctions *and, but, or, so, for*, and *yet* can combine independent clauses into compound sentences. Except when short clauses are combined and there is no confusion about meaning, a comma is used to separate the two clauses. If the subjects of the two clauses are identical, the second can be omitted and the comma avoided.

I caught the ball and I gave a cheer. (short clauses)
The music suddenly stopped, and the dancers let out a disappointed groan. (different subjects)

We agreed to sing in the chorus, but we weren't happy with the decision. (same subjects)
We agreed to sing in the chorus but weren't happy with the decision. (same subjects, one omitted)

Dad waved as she drove off, yet he worried that her experience as a driver was limited. (same subject)
Dad waved as she drove off yet worried that her experience as a driver was limited. (same subject, one omitted)

Commas are used to separate appositives from the rest of the sentence:

The mechanic, the man stretched out under the car, is nearly seventy years old.
He bought the pups, the ones that have no pedigree at all, for his children.

Commas are used to separate groups of three numbers in long numbers:

440,250   1,899,060

Use commas to separate introductory expressions, exclamations, and the names of persons directly addressed:

Well, you seem to have made yourself right at home.
Yes, I plan to stay here for a while.

As a matter of fact, I belong to the same club.
Mr. Todd, have you met my husband yet?

Commas are used in addresses to separate cities from states, in dates to separate the day from the month, and in friendly letters to end the salutation and the closing.

Centralia, Illinois   St. Louis, Missouri
New York, New York   Miami, Florida

June 10, 1960   July 4, 1776
November 11, 1918   January 1, 2009

Dear Uncle Joe,   Sincerely yours,

A title following a person's name is separated by commas from the name and the rest of the sentence.

I received the information from Helen Jones, Ph.D.
Please contact Richard Burns, M.D., at the following number.

The Colon

The colon is used to introduce information, especially when that information appears in a list:

John needed groceries again: a loaf of bread, a gallon of milk, fixings
    for a salad, and a couple of baking potatoes.

Often, a complete sentence provides the information introduced by the colon. In such a case, the first word of the sentence may or may not be capitalized. However, if multiple complete sentences provide the information, the first word following the colon should be capitalized. If an incomplete sentence follows the colon, the first word is not capitalized.

The mayor's statement made no one happy: The city must raise taxes to
    repair the streets and bridges. The fees for city services will also
    have to be raised.
What the mayor wanted was no surprise: higher taxes and fewer ser-
    vices for the citizens.

A colon is also used in the salutation of a business letter and to separate the hour from the minutes in time:

4:15 P.M.   11:45 A.M.
Dear Ms. Brown: To Whom It May Concern:

The Semicolon

The semicolon is used to suggest a lengthy pause between ideas—longer than a comma would suggest. However, there is usually a link of meaning between the ideas of the sentences combined by the semicolon:

> She became aware that the letter was not from Jim; the signature was all wrong.
> He had forgotten how to smile; two years in prison had made him a bitter man.

Parentheses

Parentheses are placed in a sentence where additional information is provided that is not essential to the meaning of the sentence:

> Her explanation on the subject is found in Chapter Ten (pages 130–139).
> Our worst winter (and hopefully, the last such winter) was in 2005.
> The Third Reich (1933–1945) changed Germany and Europe forever.

Brackets

Brackets are used to place additional information inside a parenthetical phrase:

> During the War of 1812 (President James Madison [1751–1836]), the executive mansion was set ablaze by the British.

The Apostrophe

The apostrophe has two primary functions: it is used in contractions and identifies singular and plural possessives.

> cannot → can't
> I would → I'd
> the boy's dog
> the girls' bedrooms

The Hyphen

The hyphen is used to syllabify a word at the end of a line:

... of his young daugh-   ... to win the con-
   ter and wife   test tonight

It is also used to combine words into phrases (often as modifiers)

my ten-year-old niece

The Dash

The dash may look similar to a hyphen, but it has a different function: it tells the reader of a sentence that the writer is inserting a sudden idea that is pertinent to the meaning of the sentence.

> John was so happy to move into his first apartment–the place that was all his alone.
> It was finally summer again–the season of freedom from school and of hours of fishing at the creek.

It also identifies a length of time from one date to another or a series of pages:

World War I (1914–1918)
Chapter Five (pages 93–99)

Quotation Marks

Quotation marks identify a direct quote—the actual words spoken by a person and written in a sentence. They are also used to name the title of a story.

> Mr. Will said, "This is the best steak I've ever eaten."
> Marie asked shyly, "Are you sure this is really what you want to do, sir?"
> Have you ever read "The Ransom of Red Chief?"

Single quotation marks identify a quote within a quote:

> "Bill said, 'I want nothing to do with him,' and turned away," explained Professor Smith.
> Tina said, "I recently read 'A Country Cottage' by Chekhov."

Appendix A
Verb Tables

1. The Regular Present Tense

Pronoun	*to look*	*to listen*
I	look	listen
you	look	listen
he/she/it	looks	listens
we	look	listen
you (*pl.*)	look	listen
they	look	listen

2. The Regular Present Tense: Stem Ending with *-s/-sh*

Pronoun	*to miss*	*to wash*
I	miss	wash
you	miss	wash
he/she/it	misses	washes
we	miss	wash
you (*pl.*)	miss	wash
they	miss	wash

3. The Regular Present Tense: Stem Ending in Consonant -y

Pronoun	*to try*	*to deny*
I	try	deny
you	try	deny
he/she/it	tries	denies
we	try	deny
you (*pl.*)	try	deny
they	try	deny

4. The Present Tense: Stem Ending in Vowel -y

Pronoun	*to say*	*to employ*
I	say	employ
you	say	employ
he/she/it	says	employs
we	say	employ
you (*pl.*)	say	employ
they	say	employ

5. The Present Tense: Stem Ending in Vowel -o

Pronoun	*to go*	*to do*
I	go	do
you	go	do
he/she/it	goes	does
we	go	do
you (*pl.*)	go	do
they	go	do

6. The Present Tense: Modal Auxiliaries

Pronoun	*can*	*should*	*to be able to*	*to want to*
I	can	should	am able to	want to
you	can	should	are able to	want to
he/she/it	can	should	is able to	wants to
we	can	should	are able to	want to
you (*pl.*)	can	should	are able to	want to
they	can	should	are able to	want to

7. The Present Tense: Progressive or Incomplete

Pronoun	to be	to carry	to talk
I	am being	am carrying	am talking
you	are being	are carrying	are talking
he/she/it	is being	is carrying	is talking
we	are being	are carrying	are talking
you (pl.)	are being	are carrying	are talking
they	are being	are carrying	are talking

8. The Irregular Present Tense

Pronoun	to be	to have
I	am	have
you	are	have
he/she/it	is	has
we	are	have
you (pl.)	are	have
they	are	have

9. The Regular Past Tense

Pronoun	to call	to ask
I	called	asked
you	called	asked
he/she/it	called	asked
we	called	asked
you (pl.)	called	asked
they	called	asked

10. The Irregular Past Tense: Vowel Change

Pronoun	to grow	to fall
I	grew	fell
you	grew	fell
he/she/it	grew	fell
we	grew	fell
you (pl.)	grew	fell
they	grew	fell

11. The Irregular Past Tense: Consonant Change/ Consonant Vowel Change

Pronoun	*to send*	*to do*
I	sent	did
you	sent	did
he/she/it	sent	did
we	sent	did
you (*pl.*)	sent	did
they	sent	did

12. The Irregular Past Tense: Radical Change

Pronoun	*to go*	*to be*
I	went	was
you	went	were
he/she/it	went	was
we	went	were
you (*pl.*)	went	were
they	went	were

13. The Irregular Past Tense: Full Stem Change

Pronoun	*to catch*	*to think*
I	caught	thought
you	caught	thought
he/she/it	caught	thought
we	caught	thought
you (*pl.*)	caught	thought
they	caught	thought

14. The Past Tense: Modal Auxiliaries

Pronoun	*can*	*should*	*to be able to*	*to have to*
I	could	should have	was able to	had to
you	could	should have	were able to	had to
he/she/it	could	should have	was able to	had to
we	could	should have	were able to	had to
you (*pl.*)	could	should have	were able to	had to
they	could	should have	were able to	had to

15. The Past Tense: Progressive or Incomplete

Pronoun	*to be*	*to carry*	*to talk*
I	was being	was carrying	was talking
you	were being	were carrying	were talking
he/she/it	was being	was carrying	was talking
we	were being	were carrying	were talking
you (*pl.*)	were being	were carrying	were talking
they	were being	were carrying	were talking

16. The Present and Past Perfect Tense of Regular Verbs

Pronoun	*to play*	*to try*
I	have/had played	have/had tried
you	have/had played	have/had tried
he/she/it	has/had played	has/had tried
we	have/had played	have/had tried
you (*pl.*)	have/had played	have/had tried
they	have/had played	have/had tried

17. The Irregular Present and Past Perfect Tenses: Participles Ending in *-t*

Pronoun	*to keep*	*to sleep*	*to feel*
I	have/had kept	have/had slept	have/had felt
you	have/had kept	have/had slept	have/had felt
he/she/it	has/had kept	has/had slept	has/had felt
we	have/had kept	have/had slept	have/had felt
you (*pl.*)	have/had kept	have/had slept	have/had felt
they	have/had kept	have/had slept	have/had felt

18. The Irregular Present and Past Perfect Tenses: Participles Ending in *-en*

Pronoun	*to break*	*to take*
I	have/had broken	have/had taken
you	have/had broken	have/had taken
he/she/it	has/had broken	has/had taken

we	have/had broken	have/had taken
you (*pl.*)	have/had broken	have/had taken
they	have/had broken	have/had taken

19. The Irregular Present and Past Perfect Tenses: Varied Participle Endings

Pronoun	*to go*	*to find*	*to put*	*to ring*
I	have/had gone	have/had found	have/had put	have/had rung
you	have/had gone	have/had found	have/had put	have/had rung
he/she/it	has/had gone	has/had found	has/had put	has/had rung
we	have/had gone	have/had found	have/had put	have/had rung
you (*pl.*)	have/had gone	have/had found	have/had put	have/had rung
they	have/had gone	have/had found	have/had put	have/had rung

20. The Present and Past Perfect Tenses: Progressive or Incomplete

Pronoun	*to make*	*to say*
I	have/had been making	have/had been saying
you	have/had been making	have/had been saying
he/she/it	has/had been making	has/had been saying
we	have/had been making	have/had been saying
you (*pl.*)	have/had been making	have/had been saying
they	have/had been making	have/had been saying

21. The Future Tense

Pronoun	*to hope*	*to speak*
I*	will hope	will speak
you	will hope	will speak
he/she/it	will hope	will speak
we*	will hope	will speak
you (*pl.*)	will hope	will speak
they	will hope	will speak

*In formal style, *shall* replaces *will*.

22. The Future Tense: Progressive or Incomplete

Pronoun	*to go*	*to try*
I*	will be going	will be trying
you	will be going	will be trying
he/she/it	will be going	will be trying
we*	will be going	will be trying
you (*pl.*)	will be going	will be trying
they	will be going	will be trying

*In formal style, *shall* replaces *will*.

23. The Future Perfect Tense

Pronoun	*to look*	*to break*
I*	will have looked	will have broken
you	will have looked	will have broken
he/she/it	will have looked	will have broken
we*	will have looked	will have broken
you (*pl.*)	will have looked	will have broken
they	will have looked	will have broken

*In formal style, *shall* replaces *will*.

24. The Future Perfect Tense: Progressive or Incomplete

Pronoun	*to go*	*to say*
I*	will have been going	will have been saying
you	will have been going	will have been saying
he/she/it	will have been going	will have been saying
we*	will have been going	will have been saying
you (*pl.*)	will have been going	will have been saying
they	will have been going	will have been saying

*In formal style, *shall* replaces *will*.

25. The Present Subjunctive

Pronoun	*to be*	*to have*	*to go*	*to talk*
I	be	have	go	talk
you	be	have	go	talk
he/she/it	be	have	go	talk
we	be	have	go	talk
you (*pl.*)	be	have	go	talk
they	be	have	go	talk

26. The Past Subjunctive

Pronoun	*to be*	*to have*	*to go*	*to talk*
I	were	had	went	talked
you	were	had	went	talked
he/she/it	were	had	went	talked
we	were	had	went	talked
you (*pl.*)	were	had	went	talked
they	were	had	went	talked

27. The Past Subjunctive: *would*

Pronoun	*to be*	*to say*
I	would be	would say
you	would be	would say
he/she/it	would be	would say
we	would be	would say
you (*pl.*)	would be	would say
they	would be	would say

28. The Passive Voice

Pronoun	*to be helped*	*to be seen*	*to be taken*
I	am helped	am seen	am taken
you	are helped	are seen	are taken
he/she/it	is helped	is seen	is taken
we	are helped	are seen	are taken
you (*pl.*)	are helped	are seen	are taken
they	are helped	are seen	are taken

29. The Passive Voice: Progressive or Incomplete

Pronoun	*to be helped*	*to be seen*	*to be taken*
I	am being helped	am being seen	am being taken
you	are being helped	are being seen	are being taken
he/she/it	is being helped	is being seen	is being taken
we	are being helped	are being seen	are being taken
you (*pl.*)	are being helped	are being seen	are being taken
they	are being helped	are being seen	are being taken

30. The Passive Voice: Various Tenses

Examples in the third-person singular:

Tense	*to be announced*	*to be left*
present	it is announced	it is left
present progressive	it is being announced	it is being left
past	it was announced	it was left
past progressive	it was being announced	it was being left
present perfect	it has been announced	it has been left
past perfect	it had been announced	it had been left
future	it will be announced	it will be left

31. The Imperative

Command Type	*to be*	*to find*	*to have*
you	Be	Find	Have
you (*pl.*)	Be	Find	Have
let's	Let's be	Let's find	Let's have

Appendix B
Principal Parts of Irregular Verbs

Base Form	Simple Past Tense	Past Participle
awake	awoke	awoken
be	was/were	been
	(Present tense: am/is/are)	
bear	bore	born
beat	beat	beat/beaten
become	became	become
begin	began	begun
bend	bent	bent
beset	beset	beset
bet	bet	bet
bid	bid/bade	bid/bidden
bind	bound	bound
bite	bit	bitten
bleed	bled	bled
blow	blew	blown
break	broke	broken
breed	bred	bred
bring	brought	brought
broadcast	broadcast	broadcast
build	built	built
burn	burned/burnt	burned/burnt
burst	burst	burst
buy	bought	bought
cast	cast	cast
catch	caught	caught
choose	chose	chosen
cling	clung	clung
come	came	come

Base Form	Simple Past Tense	Past Participle
cost	cost	cost
creep	crept	crept
cut	cut	cut
deal	dealt	dealt
dig	dug	dug
dive	dived/dove	dived
do	did	done
draw	drew	drawn
dream	dreamed/dreamt	dreamed/dreamt
drink	drank	drunk
drive	drove	driven
eat	ate	eaten
fall	fell	fallen
feed	fed	fed
feel	felt	felt
fight	fought	fought
find	found	found
fit	fit	fit
flee	fled	fled
fling	flung	flung
fly	flew	flown
forbid	forbade	forbidden
forget	forgot	forgotten
forego/forgo	forewent/forwent	foregone/forgone
forgive	forgave	forgiven
forsake	forsook	forsaken
freeze	froze	frozen
get	got	gotten
give	gave	given
go	went	gone
grind	ground	ground
grow	grew	grown
hang	hung	hung
hear	heard	heard
hide	hid	hidden
hit	hit	hit
hold	held	held
hurt	hurt	hurt
keep	kept	kept
kneel	knelt	knelt
knit	knit	knit
know	knew	known

Base Form	Simple Past Tense	Past Participle
lay	laid	laid
lead	led	led
leap	leaped/leapt	leaped/leapt
learn	learned/learnt	learned/learnt
leave	left	left
lend	lent	lent
let	let	let
lie	lay	lain
light	lighted/lit	lighted
lose	lost	lost
make	made	made
mean	meant	meant
meet	met	met
misspell	misspelled	misspelled
mistake	mistook	mistaken
mow	mowed	mowed/mown
overcome	overcame	overcome
overdo	overdid	overdone
overtake	overtook	overtaken
overthrow	overthrew	overthrown
pay	paid	paid
plead	pled	pled
prove	proved	proved/proven
put	put	put
quit	quit	quit
read	read	read
rid	rid	rid
ride	rode	ridden
ring	rang	rung
rise	rose	risen
run	ran	run
saw	sawed	sawed/sawn
say	said	said
see	saw	seen
seek	sought	sought
sell	sold	sold
send	sent	sent
set	set	set
sew	sewed	sewed/sewn
shake	shook	shaken
shave	shaved	shaved/shaven
shear	shore	shorn

Base Form	Simple Past Tense	Past Participle
shed	shed	shed
shine	shone	shone
shoe	shoed	shoed/shod
shoot	shot	shot
show	showed	shown
shrink	shrank	shrunk
shut	shut	shut
sing	sang	sung
sink	sank	sunk
sit	sat	sat
slay	slew	slain
sleep	slept	slept
slide	slid	slid
sling	slung	slung
slit	slit	slit
smite	smote	smitten
sow	sowed	sowed/sown
speak	spoke	spoken
speed	sped	sped
spend	spent	spent
spill	spilled/spilt	spilled/spilt
spin	spun	spun
spit	spit/spat	spit
split	split	split
spread	spread	spread
spring	sprang/sprung	sprung
stand	stood	stood
steal	stole	stolen
stick	stuck	stuck
sting	stung	stung
stink	stank	stunk
stride	strode	stridden
strike	struck	struck
string	strung	strung
strive	strove	striven
swear	swore	sworn
sweep	swept	swept
swell	swelled	swelled/swollen
swim	swam	swum
swing	swung	swung
take	took	taken
teach	taught	taught

Base Form	Simple Past Tense	Past Participle
tear	tore	torn
tell	told	told
think	thought	thought
throw	threw	thrown
thrust	thrust	thrust
tread	trod	trodden
understand	understood	understood
uphold	upheld	upheld
upset	upset	upset
wake	woke	woken
wear	wore	worn
weave	weaved/wove	weaved/woven
wed	wed	wed
weep	wept	wept
win	won	won
wind	wound	wound
withhold	withheld	withheld
withstand	withstood	withstood
wring	wrung	wrung
write	wrote	written

Index